The Complete Guide to Music Marketing

2025 Edition

By David Verney Mmus
BA Hons, FdA, CertHE

Go through the book chapter by chapter along with me, the author, in a weekly course where you can ask me all of your burning questions about music marketing. Learn more at...

https://www.patreon.com/KrannakenMusicBlog

Sixth Edition: 2025

© David Verney 2024

Contents

Acknowledgements
Praise for the Author
Introduction to the Author
Introduction to the Book

Chapter 1: Planning for Your Music Business	1
Chapter 2: Offline Music Marketing Strategies	20
Chapter 3: Offline Networking	28
Chapter 4: Online Networking	32
Chapter 5: Your Artist Website	42
Chapter 6: Stock Music	48
Chapter 7: Submitting Music to DJ Pools	61
Chapter 8: Blogging	67
Chapter 9: Artificial Intelligence	91
Chapter 10: Social Media	167
Chapter 11: Being an Independent Artist Versus Being Signed to a Label	192
Chapter 12: Distribution Channels	199
Chapter 13: Websites For Musicians	204
Chapter 14: Other Ways for Music Artists to Make Money	217
Chapter 15: Further Learning	224
Conclusion	261

Copyright © 2024 by David Verney

All rights reserved. This book or any portion thereof may not be reproduced or used in any manner whatsoever without the express written permission of the publisher except for the use of brief quotations in a book review.

Acknowledgements

There are a lot of people I can mention here. Firstly, as a Christian, I should thank God for the gift of music. I believe the pursuit of the perfect track will be never-ending.

I also need to thank my family. My wife, Catherine, is an ever-present support and always provides me with the encouragement I need to get me out of bed in the morning. My son, Connor, is a big reason for me to provide some sort of support to both my wife and my son.

I also want to thank my bandmate and best friend, Everhald for his encouragement and ever positive attitude. Everhald is a prime example of someone who excels in the face of adversity. You would think that someone who is partially deaf wouldn't be able to make great music, but several people have proved people wrong and Everhald is an example. His musical ability and skill is outstanding.

Thanks go to Alex Genadinik, my friend and business mentor. Thank you for your expert advice and for writing such a great foreword, Alex.

Without the support of any of the above people, I may well be worse off as far as my musical education goes.

I want to thank three people who I will not see again in this life. They are my parents and also Marie Fredriksson. Thank you, Mum and Dad, for being such fantastic support and putting up with me. When I look back I see times that I am not proud of. However, I am on the right track and I look forward to meeting you again in Heaven.

Marie Fredriksson, you and Per Gessle are my biggest musical inspiration of all time. I would never have picked up a guitar 30 years ago if it weren't for you. I hope you rest in peace, Marie and I hope that I will get the chance to meet with you and get to know you better in Heaven.

Thank you too, dear readers, for giving me a chance to show you something of music marketing. My plans for 2025 are to build The Complete Guide to Music Marketing into a video course that will be shared on Udemy. However, subscribers to Krannaken TV can get most of the greatest content for free because I will mention elsewhere in this book, music marketing is an ever-changing arena so this book will require further revisions on an annual basis.

Praise for the Author

David Verney is a passionate lifelong student of music and online marketing. He is also a kind individual. This book comes from his heart and marries these three notes from his background to help other aspiring musicians accomplish what they desire the most - for more people to experience their music.

David presents music marketing in a clear and structured manner, covering everything any musician needs to promote his or her music. After reading this book, any beginner music marketer will feel more confident about what they need to do and have the steps to begin promotion.

Thank you, David, for sharing your experience in this book.

Alex Genadinik
Top 1% Instructor in
Business and Marketing
on Udemy

David Verney is an exceptional digital marketing professional with a deep understanding of content creation, SEO and blog writing. His 30-year-long experience in the music industry, combined with his sharp digital marketing acumen, makes him a valuable asset in today's rapidly evolving digital landscape.

David's ability to blend traditional marketing principles with cutting-edge digital strategies showcases his adaptability and forward-thinking approach. His expertise in blog writing and content creation, particularly in the context of the music industry, is truly impressive.

David's commitment to staying ahead of industry trends, evidenced by his proficiency in leveraging AI tools for marketing, sets him apart as a thought leader in digital marketing. Any organisation looking for insightful, innovative digital marketing strategies would greatly benefit from David's consultancy services.

Neel Mistry
Career Skills Coach
Althaus Digital

Introduction to the Author

I live with my wife, Catherine and son, Connor, in the UK. My faith is one of the most important and cherished things to me and this has allowed me to build on my musical skills as a guitarist, pianist, harmonica player and producer.

As one half of the EDM duo, Krannaken, I come up with the ideas and then send them on to my bandmate, Everhald, to work his magic. Although, some work is all me or all Everhald, we do collaborate on a lot of different projects.

As well as the practical side of music, I also blog and share my knowledge and expertise with my readers through my blog. This can be found at krannaken.com. Here you will find my latest posts and new posts three times per week.

If you're a YouTube fan like me, you should also check out Krannaken TV where you will find all the latest blog posts turned into YouTube videos. I aim to provide those a-ha moments, resources and expert advice through the YouTube channel too. My channel can be found at the following link…

https://www.youtube.com/krannakentv

Please subscribe if you like what you find there…oh, and err - don't forget to hit the bell so that you are notified of all new YouTube videos as and when they are published.

Introduction to the Book

For the past 31 years, I have been more consistent as a musician and as a Christian. Although I don't write Christian songs, it is still a major part of my life. In 1994, I took up the guitar with the ambition of being the next Slash. However, Roxette were the biggest influence on my music education. I idolised Per Gessle. Even today, I class Roxette as my favourite band in world history. The biggest influence for Roxette were The Beatles – so I have to thank the Fab Four too.

This book started in September 2019. The main bones can be found on my blog at https://krannaken.com. The blog is the first place I post on in terms of my book. I take you on a journey through this book. The journey is the process that you can use to gain exposure, reach masses of fans, make more money and enjoy yourself in the process. Where I can I will show you how you can proceed without having to pay for expensive membership plans. However, the best ways of marketing your music involve some financial outlay. Don't worry, it won't break the bank! These methods will not cost a lot. We are talking monthly memberships of minimal financial requirements.

This book is intended to be used as a reference tool and not to be read from cover-to-cover. Therefore, I have included an easy-to-follow navigation system where you can get to any part of this book in just a couple of clicks. I hope this works better for you.

Chapter 1: Planning For Your Music Business

There is a saying in the marketing world that states, "if you fail to plan, you plan to fail". That is how crucial the planning stage is. Therefore, it does not matter how musical you are, your entrepreneurial skills are just as important. Every good musician and every musician who has ever made the big time (no matter how attractive they may be), is also a great entrepreneur.

However, another thing to remember is that it is ok to fail now and again. Many entrepreneurs talk about failing until they succeed. Indeed, as a student I have consistently botched up my school life and a section of my College education too. I wanted to be the class clown. I was an entertainer and I wanted to put a smile on every face in the class. Sadly, not everyone understood that and I was still considered to be the village idiot.

What are your goals?

What makes you want to work in music? Do you like the idea of getting rich doing something you love? Are you passionate about making music? My advice to you is that you have to be the latter. The passion for making music needs to far outweigh the idea of making money. You can make money doing anything. If you love music then you have a passion, but don't do it purely for the money. The chances are that you will be disappointed. In any case, you can get rich doing other things. Many of those are easier ways of making money too. It takes years of training to be good enough to make money in music. You can start a blog, and have money coming in within six months from now – so why not?

My goal has always been to do both blogging and music. In fact, my interest in music marketing goes back way longer than September, 2019. I have been interested in music marketing for over ten years. I am the stereotypical internet junkie and always finding out what the next fads are in internet marketing. There is always some scheme or other doing the rounds. You will find that many of them are scams, some are legitimate, but many are not worth your time or money.

The blog at https://krannaken.com is about music marketing. At the time of writing, I make regular blog posts and YouTube videos. You will find three posts on the blog and three YouTube videos on Krannaken TV every week. This is on a Monday, Wednesday and Friday. I publish the YouTube videos at 3 pm on these days and the blog posts are published at 6 pm. I would like to do more music review posts and interview posts. If this interests you and you want to feature, please email me at david@krannaken.com and let me know. I would be honoured to have you on the blog or on the YouTube channel. Alternatively, if you fancy having a go at a guest post, you are welcome to do something on-topic for Krannaken.com too. Please bear in mind that this is only at my discretion. It has to be on-topic and it has to be good. However, if you want to try your hand at writing a blog post, I would be very happy to consider it.

Working out your budget

Even if you are not very financially affluent, it is still worth planning a budget. You have to remember that with money, you can make money. If you make electronic music, you can create passive income by selling templates, sample packs, etc, on https://www.abletontemplates.net/.

It is very simple to explain what passive income is if you have little understanding of the concept. Basically, passive income is work that you do once, but can pay you over and over again. I am paid on a monthly basis from sales of my music. Sometimes, I make multiple sales of work that I made years ago.

With music marketing, you are always learning and you always need to be consistently learning. The internet is forever changing, after all. Furthermore, the internet is your biggest marketplace. If you hope to make money from music, the internet is your biggest and best opportunity.

Ok, let us get back to the subject of this chapter – working out your budget. I know I told you before that you don't need a lot of money. This is true, but you will find that a little money makes your life a lot easier. Many of the strategies contained in this book will require some financial input.

When you start to make some money back you should invest half of that money back into marketing and advertising your music. Spotify requires 200,000 plays per month of your tracks so that you can make the minimum wage level. This might sound like a lot of work for little return. You have to remember that the minimum wage is only coming from Spotify. To me, that is £1,091 per month from Spotify. There are something like 100 plus music streaming and retail websites. The £1,091 is from just one. Your music will have a knock-on effect on the other channels. Therefore, don't be surprised if you end up making £5-£10,000 per month from your music ($6,500-$13,000 per month). That is the kind of money that most people would be happy with. You also need to bear in mind that Spotify and many of the major music streaming and retail sites will also be happy to list your merchandise, giving you a much more lucrative way to make money than simply through stream generation.

Of that money, if you invest 50% back into your music marketing and advertising, you are looking at a snowball effect. The more people listen to your music, the more you will generate. It is important to know, however, that your music has to be good to have repeat listeners. If you want your listeners to hear your music, again and again, you will have to have something good for them. The good news is that the more music you make, the more you can expect to have good reception. Practice makes perfect after all.

Therefore, start with everything that you can manage to scrape together and consistently plough 50% back into marketing and advertising your music.

Back to Chapter 1 Navigation

Creating and developing your business plan

A good business plan is the most important aspect of any business. As I have already said: If you fail to plan, you plan to fail. Therefore, keeping an eye on your business with a good business plan is essential.

Not only will it enable you to see where your business has been, currently is and forecasts for the future, but a good business plan is also necessary if you hope to gain further funding from banks and other financial institutions.

So, what makes a good business plan? In this chapter, we are going to go through the different elements of your business plan and show you exactly what you need to include. Let's get started...

Your Cover Page

The cover page should include all of your contact details so that someone reading it can easily contact you if they need to. This information should include an address, telephone numbers for both your landline and your mobile (or cell) telephones and also your email address. If you have a website, you can also include the domain on your cover page.

Adding your degree abbreviations to your name can add credibility to you and make your plan more trustworthy and authentic.

Table of contents

It is vital that you make your reader's life as easy as possible. Therefore, you need to make every section easy to find. If an important investor needs to get to the financial information and they don't have much time, they will be impressed if you can tell them exactly which page they can find it on.

However, finding information quickly is only half the story. A contents page also makes your document look more professional and leaves a great impression in its style and format.

Executive Summary

Your executive summary needs to include your business name, your slogan and your elevator pitch. Just imagine you are in a lift with someone and you have just two minutes to impress them about your business. What would you say? How would you describe it? What is your unique selling proposition (USP)? Why should someone deal with you and not one of your competitors?. This is the information that you need to include in your executive summary.

Business Description

Here you need to expand on the description of your business. What is the legal structure of your business? Do you have a limited company, a public limited company? Are you a sole trader or a partnership?

If you have a limited company, your personal assets are safe and if your business goes out of business, your personal assets will be safe. Your personal assets include your house, car, etc. This, for many people, is the best way to go.

A sole trader is the most common legal structure for a one-man-band. For instance, if you are self-employed and work on your own with your own record label, you can have a sole trader legal structure.

Public limited companies are almost always the largest companies in business. There are very few Plc's in the music industry. Even the likes of EMI Records have a limited company legal structure.

A partnership is what Krannaken.com is. This is because there are two of us working together. A lot of artists are employed in this same legal structure.

You also need to mention the key people in your business description. Who works with you? Do you work on your own? You need to mention names. Say what makes these people a key part of your business? What skills, experience and qualifications do you have? Does anyone in your company have letters after their name? Please include all the degrees they have done in the past and write their name and all the credentials to date. For instance, on the cover page of this book, you will find my name and then my degrees "Mmus BA Hons FdA CertHE". These are all of my University credentials to date with the highest academic achievement at the start.

The business plan should also feature a more detailed explanation of your unique selling proposition. What makes your USP different? Why are you able to offer this? What is stopping your competitors from offering the same USP? Please note that this is a "unique" selling point.. Therefore, it has to be different from what other people are offering. If others aren't offering it, they may have tried it without success. In that case, why should you be any different?

As musicians, you can offer a lot of difference to others. Your music should always be unique. That is why your fans like your music.

- Finally, your business description also needs to include your location. Are you a touring artist? If so, where do your fans live? How do you plan to meet the demands of fans in those geographic locations? If you tour, you can play more gigs in areas where your fans are located. If you don't tour, you should include your location anyway. Very often, you will find that an investor will focus on investment opportunities in a certain geographic area. This could be the area where your business is located so it is a good idea to mention where you are.

Business Environmental Analysis

You can get much of this information from your market research. What is the market situation for your business? Why is it a good time to start your business? How can you position your music to gain maximum exposure? Perhaps you can advertise your music with in-stream YouTube video ads on other music videos in your genre. That is somewhere you can advertise and promote your music to people who already listen to similar music.

Industry Background

What is your experience in your industry? How many years have you played your instrument? What instruments do you play? Can you play multiple instruments? Do you produce, DJ or just play music on a guitar, keyboard, etc? How do you fulfil the demands of your business? Do you have any entrepreneurial experience? You should include as much information in these answers as you can.

Competitor Analysis

Do you know who your competitors are? Are they successful? Do they provide any opportunities for you to market your business? By this, I mean that you can exploit many marketing channels. Perhaps the best of these is YouTube. This is because YouTube offers you advertising placement on any channel you choose. Are there any good channels with plenty of subscribers? How many listeners do they get? Advertise on channels that play similar music and you will find more success.

There are also a number of third-party apps that will give you the very keywords your competitors use in marketing their videos for optimum success. If you can get this right, you will be able to get on the first page of YouTube. However, part of the success for your competitors is because there are plenty of people watching their videos and engaging with their content. If you can capture such engagement, there is nothing stopping you. YouTube always promotes videos with more engagement and gives them a higher priority.

You also need to do a SWOT analysis of your competition. This is Strengths, Weaknesses, Opportunities and Threats. What strengths do your competitors have? What are their weaknesses? Where can you exploit them and find opportunities to secure more business? Where can they exploit your business and take business from you? You should be taking advantage of opportunities to secure more business and take custom away from your competition. You should also be looking to strengthen your business and minimise the chances of business being taken from you by your competitors.

In order to clarify the answers from your SWOT analysis, you need to draw up a table. Make four quarters and put all the strengths in the box at the top left of the table. Your weaknesses go in the box at the top right of the table. Opportunities go in the box at the bottom left of the table. This leaves the box at the bottom right of the table where your threats should go.

Target Market

Who are your customers? What are their demographics? One great way to find this information is to use Facebook Insights. This will tell you everything you need to know about your target customer. You will be able to find their age, location, employment status, education, likes, interests, marital status, etc. From this information, you can gain a greater understanding of your customers, who they are and how you can reach them. Who listens to your music? What is the best price to set gig tickets at? What are the best venues for your music? You can even learn the best times to start and end your gigs. If you play next door to a railway station, what is the last train back to major urban areas? However, you will find that such organisations as transport links will be just as happy to find out when you finish as you are to find out the last train or bus back to the homes of your fans.

Management Summary

Who are the people at the top of your company? What is their experience, skillset and qualifications? What is their vision? Where do they see the business in three months, six months, one year, five years and ten years?

Operational Plan

What are you making in your business? Are you writing songs for your own band or act, or are you writing for music libraries? Do you write samples, loops, synth presets, templates, musical software or hardware? Are you promoting your music business with merchandise?

How do you create these products? Do you require any specific equipment? Do you require raw materials if you are making hardware musical gear?

How will you ensure that your products are created to the highest quality? Have you taken into account the legal aspects of your business? Do you know what laws and legislation govern your industry? How are you ensuring that you keep to these requirements?

Financial Plan

How much does it cost to create one of your products? What are the costs of labour? Do you need to spend a lot on raw materials? How much do you need to budget for marketing? What if one marketing channel does not provide sufficient results? Is your business financially viable?

You also need to create a spreadsheet that will list all your income and expenditure on a monthly basis for a three-year period. As you proceed with your business you need to constantly work on the spreadsheet. This is what is known as the Cash Flow Forecast. It enables you to see where you will be at over a period of three years or so.

With your Cash Flow Forecast, you should take into account the seasons. What are people buying and when? Are people looking for Christmas gifts for family or friends? Are they looking for a night out? Would it be a good idea to do a more festive gig before Christmas? Are you expecting more income on the run-up to Christmas? How about after Christmas? Can you ensure that people will keep buying your merchandise, products, tickets, etc, in January or February? Many businesses see a slow start to the new year after a mad and frantic run-up to Christmas. Furthermore, many shops start getting ready for Christmas in August/September.

Achievements and Milestones

What have you achieved with your music so far? How many number one hits have you had on different charts? This can include charts like Reverbnation, SoundCloud, Beatport and Hypeddit. What music qualifications do you have? What business success have you achieved so far with this business?

Creating and Developing Your Marketing Plan

Although in many cases this is included with the Business Plan, it is one of the most vital aspects of your plan. Therefore, I believe it warrants its own chapter. What is a marketing plan? Well, this is the plan that you are going to follow in order to generate your business.

Marketing is defined as everything a business does to meet the demands of the market. However, many people just see marketing as the distribution process. This process is the main part of marketing, but understanding and implementing the demands of the market is also counted as marketing. Therefore, market research is the first part of marketing that you will need to conduct before you proceed to other areas.

How are you going to conduct market research? Which service are you going to use to conduct your questionnaire? Are you going to offer an incentive to people who complete your market research questionnaire?

A few years ago, conducting an online market research questionnaire was an expensive business. There was only one service that required a payment of around £200 in order to use it. Today, however, we have Google Forms so the rest is history..

When you have the results of your market research, you can tailor your product to the requirements of your audience. This enables you to meet demand and generate a good, solid and professional image and reputation for your company as one of the pioneers of your industry.

Distribution of Your Product

Ok, so we have looked at the pre-production stage. Now let's look at what you have been waiting for, the distribution stage.

How are you going to meet the demands of your customers and find the very people your product is aimed at? It is no good aiming metal music at a dance music festival. Therefore, you need the right kind of music fan.

Many younger producers will stick to hip-hop, thinking that their songs are good enough for chart success. However, these people want to be like someone. They want to be just like Eminem, for example. The thing is, is that you have to make your own sound. You have to find your own unique sound. What genres of music are you most interested in creating? People will want to be like you because you are different.

It used to take 80,000 monthly streams to generate the equivalent of the minimum wage on Spotify. Nowadays, you are looking at somewhere closer to 200,000 streams. How are you going to generate that many streams? People are not going to listen to you if you sound like someone else. What is the point in us sounding like Armin Van Buuren if people only want to listen to Armin Van Buuren? They will listen to Armin, not us. Therefore, we have to be different. We have to make our own sound and it has to be good. You have to be a pioneer and forge new sounds that will generate significant interest in the fans you have already, and also in new potential fans.

Anyway, let's get back to the subject of distribution. How are you going to find your fans? The great thing is that the internet makes this easy. It means you can advertise on sites like Facebook and find the very people who are interested in playing, purchasing and promoting your music. Perhaps the best of these sites for targeting is Facebook. We can find out exactly who our fans are and target them directly through the power of Facebook.. Not only is Facebook great for targeting, it is also great because we can generate interest for a few pence per listen. This means you can find fans at a great price and have them share your music for free.
When people find music they enjoy, they are going to share it. It is as simple as that. A fan will buy your music, they will wear your merchandise. Therefore, a fan becomes an advertisement for you in the process.

Wherever you are advertising, it is always a good idea to split test your advertisements to ensure you have the best results from your advertising. Split testing allows you to advertise the same product in two different images, different wording or different font styles, sizes or colours. Once you have found the optimum layout, wording etc, you can proceed with this advertisement and generate product sales with greater success.

As musicians, you need to be heard for people to actually take note of your music. Therefore, you are better to advertise on sites like YouTube and SoundCloud because people get a taste for your music as a result.

You should also use Hypeddit with SoundCloud. These two go hand in hand. You can generate a lot of SoundCloud fans if you use Hypeddit. Hypeddit aids in providing a free download on SoundCloud because people who want to download your track have to share your music in any or any number of 12 different social media and music streaming sites.

Marketing Budget

Although you need to generate 200,000 streams of your music on Spotify before you get the equivalent of the minimum wage, you can imagine how much we are generating from other channels. There are over 100 more music streaming and retail websites on the internet. If you get the minimum wage from one of those sites, you can imagine how good it will be all together. We will be doing very well for ourselves if we can generate 80,000 Spotify plays.

It is a good idea to plough 50% of the income back into the marketing and promoting of your music or music business. If you do this, you will find that it will quickly grow and you will be generating more money as a result. This is why you need to keep it up in the studio. The more material you generate, the better you will get. The better you get, the more people will want to hear your music. The more people who hear your music, the more income you will generate.

Chapter 2: Offline Music Marketing Strategies

Although the internet represents your biggest chances of succeeding with your music, it is also essential that you make the most of your offline music marketing strategies too. This can be anything from the sale of merchandise to networking and there are a number of different strategies that you can implement to increase awareness of your music and generate more income for you in the process.

Ideas For Offline Strategies

There are plenty of ways that you can market your music offline. These include

Networking

There are now a lot of opportunities for networking. You may have experience of business networking or speed dating. The latter isn't known to be networking, but in theory that is exactly what it is. As an experienced business networker, I have found these events to be both challenging and interesting. You meet some great people who are like-minded and you build your confidence in meeting new people as a result. I have included a section on business networking later in the book so if you would like to learn more about networking, you can refer to that chapter.

Playing Gigs

If you can get a paid gig, then that is fantastic. You can gain great exposure for your music and you don't know who is in the audience. However, if you have not got a gig coming up, it may be worth you offering to do a free gig. Although you aren't being paid for a free gig, you can still get some valuable exposure for your music. You may be approached to do a paid gig during this gig. Maybe there are weddings or other events where you can perform. You may still find that your Spotify listener numbers increase as a result of you playing this show.

Selling Merchandise

Another thing you can do is ask venue employees (bar staff, etc) to sell your CDs while you are playing. The result is that both you and the venue employees will earn money.

You should always consider exposure before financial gain. You can sell CDs, T-shirts or any other merchandise in this way.

The great thing about merchandise is that it is advertising that pays you. You are earning money from merchandise sales and the merchandise advertises your music at the same time.

Companies who sell merch include Teespring, CafePress, Zazzle, Two-Fifteen, and Inkthreadable.

Advertising in Local and Regional Newspapers and Magazines

There is nothing wrong with you advertising your music in a local or regional newspaper or magazine. However, you will not need to do this if you want to play private functions such as weddings, birthday parties, etc. Also, remember that each show is an advertisement. If you perform well at one event, there is nothing stopping you being hired again as a result.

You should really target the What's On section of your local advertising magazines. When I was a boy, we had an advertising magazine every Sunday called "the Why Magazine". I was always reading it and waiting for it every Sunday so that I could see what was being advertised. I purchased several items such as video game consoles through the Why Magazine.

Contacting DJ's

If you produce electronic music, as we do, you will do well to contact nightclub, radio or mobile DJ's and ask them to play your music. We have had international air-play as a result of contacting a radio station in the USA. As we are in the UK, it is interesting to see that we get a lot of our followers from the western side of the Atlantic Ocean.

In this edition, I have also included a section on DJ record pools. These are websites where DJs go for their music. We have had some significant success as a result of submitting our music to DJ record pools. There is nothing stopping you from doing the same - especially if you make electronic music.

You can also network with DJs through networking meetings. Make sure that you have some business cards to hand out if you are going to be networking. The information on your card should include your Spotify link.

I am also in contact with different DJ's on Facebook. However, as that is online, I will save it for another section.

Another way to network with like-minded artists and DJs is through SoundCloud. This network has the biggest number of DJs following because they see it as a great way to network with other musicians, artists, gain exposure and feedback on their music and tap into a stream of new and unheard-of artists who play the kind of music they want to promote.

Handing Out Flyers and CDs

It is a good idea to purchase CDs in bulk, burn music onto them and then hand them out at networking meetings.

Maybe you could hand out CDs at a shopping centre or public transport hub. The former is probably the best place as that is where people expect to be handed flyers, etc. If you hand out a CD, that is different. People don't expect to be given CDs while they shop and the fact that it is unusual should make your offering fairly popular.

Another factor in favour of CDs is the curiosity factor. What does the music sound like? Will people like it? This curiosity factor should have people playing your music. If you hand out a flyer with it to explain where they can get or download your music, there is nothing stopping further interest.

Pinning Flyers and Posters to Noticeboards

Depending on the noticeboards, you can get away with pinning posters and flyers to noticeboards for free. A few years ago, I pinned a flyer to a noticeboard at Coventry University for free and got some business as a result.

There are more prominent places to pin flyers and posters. You will find many newsagents will charge a minimal amount to advertise your poster or flyer. Some of these shops are next to bus stops etc. If you find such a shop, you really need to take advantage of this opportunity.

I found a job through advertising my services on a shop noticeboard. This particular employment lasted for six years. That was a good return for such a cheap investment. It was my wife's suggestion to advertise in that shop window.

Using Car Magnets

If you, a family member or close friend drive cars, there is nothing wrong with requesting that they place a car magnet on their doors. Such magnets will advertise your music and after a while, you just forget they are there. It takes seconds to put it on a car door and yet, whenever the car is on the move, it is advertising your music. Sometimes, a car can be in a busy road. The other thing to remember here is that many people listen to music while they are driving. If someone sees your car magnet while they are playing Spotify, there is a good chance that they will investigate your music out of pure curiosity.

Using Your Tribe

If your friends and family are in support of your music, they will be willing to help however they can. Therefore, they will show your music to their friends, families and acquaintances. A group of people who promote the work of someone, or a group of people, are known as a tribe. Your tribe are fans of you and your music and they will be happy to promote you however they can and however you can suggest.

I first heard of the concept of tribal marketing when writing my blog. Everybody shares everybody else's content if they can and if it fits in with their other content. I haven't ever spoken orally to any of these people, but over the past month, I had a reach of almost 3 million people. We will talk about this further in another chapter.

Playing Music in Public Places

This is one thing my brother is always doing. He will get on a bus and play music out loud. As he is mainly into 1980s music, he will play this without worrying about what other people may think. He has also played my music out loud on the bus which was a proud moment.

The thing to remember here is that you are gaining exposure for your music by playing it in public places. People may be wondering what it is, what it is called, who it is by, etc. For all we know, someone could be sitting there with an app like Shazam and discover more about the track being played.

Chapter 3: Offline Networking

Although this is probably going to be one of the shortest chapters in the book, it is nonetheless an important one so it is well worth inclusion. Whatever kind of life you have, there will always be reason to socialise.

It does not matter if you are the most introverted person in the world, you will find a reason to mix with others. If you are an introvert, you may well need to find a group to become more of an extrovert. Therefore, the group would be more of a self-development and self-help group that would be made up of people just like yourself.

I have been active in business networking quite extensively in the past. One was a Christian networking group called Training Kings. The others were general entrepreneurship groups, but Training Kings was the one I became most involved with.

I found that I could meet new people and make new friends, many of whom I still correspond with today – several years after Training Kings went out of business. Another good thing about such a group is that I became more confident and more sociable as a result of my membership and participation in group meetings. I also found that I actually enjoy public speaking because of my experience with Training Kings.

Benefits of Offline Networking Groups For Musicians

There are many benefits of membership and participation in such groups. Not only spending time in the company of like-minded individuals. These people can become great friends as I have experienced myself from my networking experience.

Other benefits of offline networking groups for musicians can include, but are no way limited to the following…

- We can find other musicians to work with. If we need to find a saxophonist, a harmonica player or we want to use a real drum kit, we can find these people in this type of group.
- I have personally found opportunities for new musical projects to work on from someone in Training Kings. Please note that TK is not a music networking group at all. The lady just needed someone who could put poetry to music for her.
- You may be able to help someone else by introducing someone you know to them.
- It is possible to find record contracts, marketing promotion, merchandising opportunities, funding and lots of other types of marketing and promotion through such groups.

- Just as with me, practising my elevator pitch every month made me more confident and I was able to speak in front of large hotel function rooms in front of an audience. Think about this one. If you lack confidence and want to perform in front of an audience, this one can really help a lot.

- Such groups include training and educational presentations. Training Kings did not call itself "Training" for the sake of it. These guys really did treat their members like Kings too. I built my confidence until I was able to get up and do a presentation in front of the audience on my own.

- You can often get a meal there. With Training Kings, we had breakfast. The meetings would go on from 7.30am to 9.30am so breakfast was in demand. Plus events were held at hotels where breakfast was available. So, why not take advantage.

The Best Two Organisations Who Provide Networking Groups For Musicians

Meetup: https://www.meetup.com/

Meetup are the biggest and best place to find networking groups in your area. These will be both performance, production and appreciation groups. Therefore, you should be able to find something local to where you are that is just what you are looking for.

Eventbrite: https://www.eventbrite.co.uk/

When you look for Eventbrite, you are better to go to Google and do a search for Eventbrite in your country. For me, I use the .co.uk site because I'm British. If you are an American, you may wonder why my spelling is off. It is quite simply because I write in British English (the original is always the best).

When you first go on the website of Eventbrite, you will be presented with a search box. If you type "music" in the box and hit enter. You will then be given a list of events that are in your area. For instance, I am presented with a list of groups in Birmingham and Wolverhampton. These, again, are a mixture of different types of groups. There is anything from musical performance groups to musical therapy. The groups tend to be listed with the headlines of what is actually going to happen at the group.

Chapter 4: Online Networking

If you are going to start a music business, you will find the internet invaluable for meeting new people, finding new projects, opportunities and everyone else who may be able to help in your projects. Your projects quickly become their projects too. So, why is online networking so important for today's recording artist?

Benefits of Online Networking

The most obvious benefit of online networking is that you are not tied by geographic location. If you find out there is an offline networking event in New York or Los Angeles and you live in London, you are hardly going to jump on a plane to get there unless you have sufficient finance and motivation to go. Whereas, if you are online and are attending a networking event on Google Meet or Zoom, you can be on the opposite side of the world and the only financial consideration you have to take on board is your time. How much are you paid each hour? Is the event financially worth your time? Many events will take place at night after you finish your daily work. If this is the case for you, it may be a good investment of your time.

Other benefits include the fact that you don't have to spare as much time as you do in offline networking. You only really have to spare the actual hours of the event. When I was attending Training Kings events, I would get up two hours before the event started.

Therefore, I was up at 5.30am to get to the event for 7.30 am. It was more fun to attend the event offline, but the hours it took out of my day were double the time that I took in attending online meetings.

Geographic location also affects numbers of attendees4. Every Facebook group that you are a member of is essentially, a networking community. It is a community of people who help one another. There are similar communities on other websites too, but Facebook will be the first example you can think of.

For some of my University projects in both my Foundation Degree and my Bachelor's Degree, I have had to network with other musicians and music industry professionals as a part of the module. This has included singers, drummers, guitarists and others. Facebook is the first place I would go to find the right people to work with.

If you are not a brick-and-mortar establishment and you can accept orders from anywhere in the world, online networking is ideal for your customer acquisition. The world is quite literally your oyster. You can generate business from any location in the world. This also means that you can be as remote as you like. All you need is a reliable internet connection. Unfortunately, many rural communities all over the world do not have an internet connection. However, if you are in a city or the more suburban areas of a larger city or town, you can expect to find that the area is served well by the internet. Not only that, but you can also expect that hotels, leisure centres, transport links, etc, will have broadband available (quite often free of charge). In many cases, it is essential to the success of their businesses.

If you are out of work and need to find something, online networking will allow you to sell your skills and find something that you can do. This would fit in with all your requirements. If you have to get your children to school at 9 am, you have the flexibility to start working once you get home.

You never know what other people in the group can do. For instance, maybe a guitarist or a producer in the group has experience of certain holiday destinations. They may be able to recommend hotels, airlines, tourist attractions or local food. This may turn your next holiday into something very special that you will remember for the rest of your life.

If you are unsure of a technical process, skill or if you are unfamiliar with a VST that you really want to get to grips with, you can meet people in online communities who may be able to help. However, I would advise your first port of call to be YouTube if you need any of this information.

Yet another good thing about networking is that you can learn the trends in both business processes and technology. If you need to find the right VST, hardware instrument or any other hardware or software technology, networking can enable you to keep informed of technological breakthroughs and trends. The advantage that online networking has over offline networking here is that there are a lot more people in online communities than there are offline. Therefore, you are able to be better informed of such trends.

Drawbacks of Online Networking

The biggest drawback of online networking is that we shut ourselves away from the world. Therefore, we become reclusive and this has a negative effect on our mental health. We can combat this by taking a walk around the local area every day.

There are a few other drawbacks to online networking. These include the fact that people can hide their true feelings when communicating online. You never know what people are really thinking. They can just show the emotions that they want you to see rather than their true emotions.

People can also be rude and extremely offensive without any retribution when they are communicating in an online networking group. You can think of the worst thing that someone has said and freely say it on Facebook. You can even mislead people and give them false information that they believe to be true.

Online networking also goes against the maintenance of people's communication skills. Many people have poor spelling without the need for face-to-face communication. My bandmate's written English is poor and this belies his intelligence. He has a degree in music production and is very intelligent. However, if you were judging him based on his written English, you would have a much worse opinion of him. This can be true of many people. You probably know people who are just like my friend.

Some people argue that online networking diminishes understanding and thoughtfulness. However, for me, I am much better with the written word than I am in person. In person, I might put you off. I have put off many would-be girlfriends in person. My wife gave me the benefit of the doubt. That is why we got together. I am partially sighted and thick lenses in my glasses pose a barrier to proper relationships. Some people think that thick lenses in the glasses equal learning difficulties. However, this is just so wrong. It is why only people with some intelligence are my friends – which suits me. I can have an academically intelligent conversation with true friends.

It is said that online networking also facilitates laziness. This laziness can often lead to health problems such as the mental health issues we have already mentioned. However, there are also physical issues here. If we are lazy it is easy to become obese. This, in turn, leads to a lot of additional health problems such as diabetes. It wastes muscle tissue. If we are not using our muscles, they will not strengthen. These issues are faced by many people in the music industry who will shut themselves away for hours, and in some cases, days.

List of Online Networking Sites

Here is a list of online music networking sites that you can investigate for yourself…

Music2Deal https://music2deal.com/

Music2Deal is an online networking community for music industry professionals. You will find people who work in every facet of the music industry and from all over the world. It looks like a fantastic opportunity to meet, network and befriend like-minded people from around the globe.

SoundCloud: https://soundcloud.com/

SoundCloud gives you the ability to like, chat, critique and share other artist's work. The great thing is, that many people will reciprocate and like, comment and share your music in return.

Another great feature is only available on the upgraded membership. This is called Spotlight and gives you the opportunity to showcase five tracks at the top of your artist profile.

Partyaner: https://www.partyaner.com/en/

Partyaner offers free membership and allows you to showcase your music to a growing community of music artists and fans. You also have the opportunity to follow other people, arrange collaborations, organise events and connect with all kinds of music industry professionals.

LoudUp: https://www.loudup.com/

LoudUp is another networking site that allows artists and music enthusiasts to connect.

Reverbnation: https://www.reverbnation.com/

Reverbnation is not short on unique features. This platform lists tonnes of different musical opportunities. Although one of my favourite features is the feedback that can be gained if you are looking for feedback on any track.

You can also gain a lot of exposure for your music and climb the local Reverbnation charts. Krannaken have had three number one songs on Reverbnation. One of these was Christmas 2017.

8Tracks: https://8tracks.com/

8Tracks allows you to create and promote playlists.

Groupsite.com: https://groupsite.com/

Although GroupSite is not strictly for musicians, it does support collaborative projects and this is why it is listed here. It allows communication and organisation of all kinds of collaborative projects.

Jamendo: https://www.jamendo.com/

Jamendo allows you to both promote your music to fans and also find licensing opportunities. This makes it one of the most exciting opportunities so far on this list.

Kompoz: https://www.kompoz.com/music/

On Kompoz the main function is collaboration. However, there is also an opportunity to build public and private groups of your fans and contacts.

The number of public and private collaborations and private and public groups depends on the level of your membership. You can promote up to 3 collaborations with the free account, or unlimited collaborations with the most expensive membership. The latter membership is priced at $20 per month.

However, if we were to join Kompoz ourselves, we would be fine with the $10/monthly membership plan. This would give us 72 collaborative projects per year as well as 20 private collaborations. Therefore, we would get more than one collaboration per week. For our $10, we can also create and promote up to 10 public groups and 5 private groups.

Audiodraft: https://www.audiodraft.com/careers-in-music/

Audiodraft offer the chance to create music for a diverse range of brands. This could be anything from sound effects, to voice overs, composing music and collaborating with others.

Discogs: https://www.discogs.com/

On Discogs, you have the opportunity to discover, buy and sell music. Therefore, it's worth checking out with a view to selling your music and merchandise through this platform.

Drooble: https://drooble.com/

One feature that Drooble has, that is not apparent everywhere, is that you can get paid for reviewing songs. This is an interesting way to make money. I wouldn't advise you to dump your day job just yet though. The chances are that they will not be able to provide a regular full-time or even part-time income.

Blip: https://blip.fm/

Blip is like Twitter with the only difference being that Blip embeds a song into your tweet. This site has big potential and can play just about any song on earth – including most of Krannaken's repertoire.

Hypeddit: https://hypeddit.com/

This is one that Krannaken use all the time. We can quickly build, grow our muic and share it with massive audiences on all the major social media sites.

StageIt: https://www.stageit.com/

If you are stuck without any gigs to put on at any venue, why not hold a gig at home in the comfort of your own living room? With StageIt, you can do just that. Your fans will also be able to pay you for attending the gig and also tip you while they watch you play.

Chapter 5: Your Artist Website

As the internet is your biggest market, you will need to have a web presence. Your website will keep your fans satisfied as well as reach out to new fans. In this chapter, we are going to look at your artist website and give you some ideas that you can use going forwards.

What Platform is Best For Your Artist Website?

The first consideration you should have is whether you are going to choose a website builder or build your own website through WordPress.org. I strongly advise that you pay for your website rather than having a free website such as Blogger or WordPress.com. Not only do they look unprofessional, they also require ownership of your content. Therefore, your content would never be your own.

With our Krannaken website, we pay a monthly fee of a few pounds and we get to own our own content. You can also make more money with a WordPress.org website and tailor it to your own requirements.

Website builders include Bandzoogle, Music Glue and BandVista. Don't worry, you are not inviting a bunch of smelly, dirty men with foul language to do work on your website as they would on your house. A website builder can be customised to suit your own needs. However, as I said, WordPress.org gives you ultimate control over how your website will look.

The Bandzoogle website builder (https://bandzoogle.com/) offers a range of music-services. You can sell anything you want. In my view, the biggest plus point for Bandzoogle is the email marketing service that you get with it. However, you can also get an SSL certificate thrown in.

If you are unsure of what an SSL is, it is the https:// rather than the http://. This is important because Google will not list a website without an SSL so you won't reach as many people as you need. Therefore, you are leaving a big chunk of business on the table for other bands and artists to gain custom from rather than you.

Music Glue (https://www.musicglue.com/) offer an interesting proposition. They charge 10% or 15% of your commission depending on which plan you choose when you sign up.

For the 15% plan, they have a wide range of business features rather than Bandzoogle's more music focused features. These include things like accounting, social media, etc. They do not have email marketing thrown in, but for the commission they charge, you can't expect that much.

Elements of Your Website

Choosing Your Theme

After choosing your website platform, you need to choose a theme. There are literally thousands of these. However, I would highly recommend the theme we purchased from Second Line (https://secondlinethemes.com/). They have five different WordPress themes that are all made for musicians. These look great and are available for a one-time payment of $69. I purchased mine through AppSumo for $49. I would advise you to visit AppSumo (https://appsumo.com/)

However, there are literally millions of themes available if you choose a WordPress.org website. If you use the above-mentioned website builders, you will be restricted to a much smaller choice of themes.

Email Marketing Providers

If you don't use Bandzoogle, Music Glue or BandVista, you should also look at your email marketing provider. Although email marketing is not compulsory, it is highly advisable. You have the ability to make much more money as a result of using email marketing. The biggest providers of email marketing services are Getresponse and Aweber. However, there are also free services like MailChimp. This latter service is available for free for a restricted number of emails. You can send out something like 12,000 emails per month on this free account.

Layout of your blog

The biggest goal behind your website, whether that is a music website or just a run-of-the-mill blog, is to get as much attention for your content as possible. Therefore, you need to use the "F" theory.

The "F" theory is scientifically proven to be the best way to grab the attention of your readers. It is called the "F" because your readers view your web page like an "F". Their first point of focus is at the top-left of your screen. They look across, so they will read your headline first. Then they look down the screen and they may look over a little way down the screen.

Therefore, it is vital that you make the main goal of your business, or website, the first thing people notice. If your goal is to get email sign-ups for your website, you should put the reason why people should sign up at the top of your website, with the actual email opt-in box next to it, in the top right corner.

Another aspect to consider is your type of media. Are you using video, audio or just basic text. As a musician, I expect that you are using audio. Therefore, you should use an audio player on your post. If you are using Second Line, they have the audio player plugin already installed.

If you use one of the other website builders I have already mentioned, you probably get an audio player along with it. However, if you just want to play audio, you can just enter your code in your posts and you will be embedding your video in your blog post.

Outsourcing Your Website Design

Most website builders are easy and straightforward to understand. WordPress.org is likewise. However, there may still be things that are less easy to do. For instance, you may be required to do a minimal amount of coding to install certain plugins. If this is the case and you are either unsure of the technology, or if you are technophobic, you can outsource the work for a minimal charge and have an experienced professional do the work for you.

You can find inexpensive rates for doing such work on sites like Fiverr. In fact, I suggest you try Fiverr first and foremost. This is because charges are lower on Fiverr than you may be expected to pay on other freelance websites.

In its early days, Fiverr was called fiverr because everything was just $5. You couldn't charge more or less for your services. This gave people a good understanding that the site was inexpensive and you could get a job done for $5. However, today, the site allows merchants to charge much more with the base rate being at $5. Fiverr charges the customer a little extra (something like 10% extra) to cover their charges.

Chapter 6: Stock Music

What is Stock Music

Have you ever wondered where videos, games, TV programs, radio adverts, social media adverts, etc, etc, etc, get their music from? Let me introduce you to the world of stock music composition.

As a stock music composer, you create the music, upload your music to various different non-exclusive libraries or just one exclusive library. These sites are high-trafic and they generate a lot of interest and a lot of sales from people who require music for the above types of media.

Pros of Being a Stock Music Composer

The life of a stock music composer is fun. You get to write the music you like and how you like it with your own unique spin.

Stock music composition can also provide you with passive income. This means that you will be paid time and again for sales of the same music. You occasionally hear of people making money while they sleep. These people are making money passively and that is what you can expect as a stock music composer.

Cons of Being a Stock Music Composer

As a stock music composer, you can never say how much you will earn in any given time period. Some tracks that you think will do well, won't sell at all. Other music that you think was poor, may sell very well. You can't say how well a piece of music will sell until it does.

What is the Difference Between Exclusive and Non-Exclusive Production Music Libraries?

If a library is exclusive, it means that you are only selling this music through that library.

Most libraries are either completely non-exclusive, or they operate both types of licenses. This means you have a lot of freedom to use your music as you would like to.

Although a non-exclusive license gives you liberty over your work, an exclusive license also means that you will be paid more per sale. Therefore, you have to ask yourself whether you want to make more sales, or whether you want to make more for an individual sale.

Libraries always list their terms and conditions, including how much they offer you of the sale as a percentage. It is important to note that, while you make great music, the libraries will also provide you with the traffic and ears to hear that music.

Therefore, it is much better to team up with them - at least in the short term.

Many composers do actually go it alone and sell from their own websites rather than through a library. While this is beneficial for established composers, it is not as good as using a library if you are a newbie.

38 Production Music Libraries

Here is a list of the top 50 production music libraries along with license types and also what media opportunities each of these is good for. I have also provided you with the website addresses for each of these libraries...

1. Audio Network

Deal Type: Exclusive
Best For: TV, Film, Advertising
https://www.audionetwork.com/

2. Pond5

Deal Type: Non-Exclusive
Best For: YouTube, Online Videos, Independent Filmmakers
https://www.pond5.com/

3. PremiumBeat

Deal Type: Exclusive
Best For: Video Productions, Commercials
https://www.premiumbeat.com/

4. Epidemic Sound

Deal Type: Non-Exclusive
Best For: YouTube, Social Media, Online Content
https://www.epidemicsound.com/

5. Artlist

Deal Type: Although Artlist are not accepting new applications at the time of writing, I will still include them because maybe they are open to new artists again when you read this.
Best For: YouTube, Social Media, Online Content
https://artlist.io/

6. Music Vine

Deal Type: Both Exclusive and Non-Exclusive
Best For: Film, TV, Advertising
https://musicvine.com/

7. AudioJungle

Deal Type: Exclusive and Non-Exclusive
Best For: Web Projects, Online Videos, Podcasts
https://audiojungle.net/

8. Shutterstock Music

Deal Type: Non-Exclusive
Best For: Advertising, Film, Online Videos
https://www.shutterstock.com/music

9. Envato Elements

Deal Type: Non-Exclusive
Best For: YouTube, Social Media, Online Content
https://elements.envato.com/

10. Jingle Punks

Deal Type: Non-Exclusive
Best For: TV, Film, Advertising
https://jinglepunks.com/

11. APM Music

Deal Type: Non-Exclusive
Best For: TV, Film, Advertising

https://www.apmmusic.com/

12. MegaTrax

Deal Type: Non-Exclusive
Best For: TV, Radio, Film
https://www.megatrax.com/

13. Killer Tracks (Universal Production Music)

Deal Type: Exclusive
Best For: TV, Film, Advertising
https://www.universalproductionmusic.com/

14. FirstCom Music

Deal Type: Exclusive
Best For: TV, Radio, Advertising
https://firstcom.com

15. AudioSparx

Deal Type: Non-Exclusive
Best For: TV, Film, Online Videos
https://www.audiosparx.com/

16. Songtradr

Deal Type: Non-Exclusive
Best For: YouTube, Online Videos, Independent Films
https://www.songtradr.com/

17. Musicbed

Deal Type: Non-Exclusive
Best For: Wedding Videos, Indie Films, Commercials
https://www.musicbed.com/

18. ScoreKeepers Music

Deal Type: Exclusive
Best For: TV, Film, Advertising
https://www.scorekeepersmusic.com/

19. West One Music

Deal Type: Exclusive
Best For: TV, Film, Advertising
https://www.westonemusic.com/

20. BeatPick

Deal Type: Non-Exclusive
Best For: Indie Films, Online Videos, Advertising
https://www.beatpick.com/

21. Soundstripe

Deal Type: Non-Exclusive
Best For: YouTube, Social Media, Online Videos
https://www.soundstripe.com/

22. Crucial Music

Deal Type: Non-Exclusive
Best For: TV, Film, Advertising
https://www.crucialmusic.com/

23. Marmoset

Deal Type: Non-Exclusive
Best For: Indie Films, Advertising, Online Videos
https://www.marmosetmusic.com/

24. AudioMicro

Deal Type: Non-Exclusive
Best For: Online Videos, Podcasts, Commercials
https://www.audiomicro.com/

25. Triple Scoop Music

Deal Type: Non-Exclusive
Best For: Wedding Videos, Indie Films, Photography Projects
https://www.triplescoopmusic.com/

26. Smartsound

Deal Type: Non-Exclusive
Best For: Video Editing, Online Videos, Commercials
https://www.smartsound.com/

27. Position Music

Deal Type: Exclusive
Best For: Trailers, TV, Film
https://www.positionmusic.com/

28. Atomica Music

Deal Type: Exclusive
Best For: TV, Film, Advertising
https://www.atomicamusic.com/

29. Extreme Music

Deal Type: Non-Exclusive
Best For: TV, Film, Advertising
https://www.extrememusic.com/

30. SoundDogs

Deal Type: Non-Exclusive
Best For: Film, TV, Online Videos
https://sounddogs.com/

31. Audiosocket

Deal Type: Exclusive and Non-Exclusive
Best For: Indie Films, Online Videos, Advertising
https://www.audiosocket.com/

32. Bedtracks

Deal Type: Non-Exclusive
Best For: TV, Film, Advertising
https://www.bedtracks.com/

33. BMG Production Music

Deal Type: Non-Exclusive
Best For: Trailers, TV, Film
https://bmgproductionmusic.com/

34. Indaba Music

Deal Type: Non-Exclusive
Best For: Online Videos, Indie Films, Advertising
https://www.indabamusic.com/

35. Uppbeat

Deal Type: Non-Exclusive
Best For: YouTube, Social Media, Online Videos
https://uppbeat.io/

36. Filmmusic.io

Deal Type: Non-Exclusive
Best For: Indie Films, Online Videos, Advertising
https://filmmusic.io/

37. Zapsplat

Deal Type: Non-Exclusive
Best For: Online Videos, Podcasts, Indie Films
https://www.zapsplat.com/

38. Storyblocks

Deal Type: Non-Exclusive
Best For: YouTube, Social Media, Online Videos
https://www.storyblocks.com/

It should be noted that some of the additions to this list may be more difficult to work with than others. For instance, AudioJungle have a very stringent acceptance rate. If you submit to AudioJungle and they decline your submission, don't worry. You need to be resilient. There is a fantastic chance that your work will be accepted by other libraries.

If you want to learn more about stock music licensing, I highly recommend Daniel Carrizalez and his YouTube channel Stock Music Licensing. You can find Daniel's YouTube channel at https://www.youtube.com/@StockMusicLicensing/videos

Chapter 7: Submitting Music to DJ Pools

As electronic music DJs, Everhald and I don't perform our music on stage. You may be asking, "how do you get exposure for your music if you don't perform?" We use DJ record pools.

DJ record pools are websites where all kinds of different DJs can download different music. We have a worldwide audience because several DJs have downloaded our music.

Over the following following few pages, I have listed no fewer than 29 DJ record pools. Some will be free. A lot of these may charge you to list your music on their website. However, there are some who only charge the DJs and some who don't take a lot of submissions. However, all of these sites are worth investigating...

List of DJ Record Pools

1. BPM Supreme

Popular Genres: Hip-hop, R&B, Pop, Dance, Electronic, Country and Rock
Types of DJs: Club DJs, Mobile DJs, Radio DJs
Website for Submissions:
https://bpmsupreme.com/submissions

2. Digital DJ Pool

Popular Genres: Top 40, Hip-hop, House, EDM, Latin
Types of DJs: Club DJs, Mobile DJs, Radio DJs, Event DJs
Website for Submissions:
https://digitaldjpool.com/music-promotion

3. DJcity

Popular Genres: Hip-hop, R&B, EDM, Latin, Pop
Types of DJs: Club DJs, Radio DJs, Event DJs
Website for Submissions:
https://support.djcity.com/hc/en-us/articles/230488708-How-do-I-get-my-music-on-DJcity

4. Club Killers

Popular Genres: Hip-hop, EDM, House, Latin, Pop
Types of DJs: Club DJs, Radio DJs, Event DJs
Website for Submissions:
https://www.clubkillers.com/submissions

5. Direct Music Service (DMS)

Popular Genres: Hip-hop, Top 40, House, Classics, Mashups
Types of DJs: Club DJs, Mobile DJs, Radio DJs, Wedding DJs
Website for Submissions:
https://www.directmusicservice.com/contact-us/

6. Late Night Record Pool

Popular Genres: Hip-hop, R&B, House, EDM, Pop
Types of DJs: Club DJs, Radio DJs, Mobile DJs
Website for Submissions:
https://www.latenightrecordpool.com/contact-us/

7. MyMP3Pool

Popular Genres: Hip-hop, R&B, Dance, Latin, Pop
Types of DJs: Club DJs, Mobile DJs, Event DJs
Website for Submissions:
https://mp3poolonline.com/

8. Franchise Record Pool

Popular Genres: Hip-hop, R&B, EDM, Reggae, Latin
Types of DJs: Club DJs, Radio DJs, Mobile DJs
Website for Submissions:
https://www.franchiserecordpool.com/contact/

9. Crate Connect

Popular Genres: Hip-hop, House, EDM, Top 40, Latin
Types of DJs: Club DJs, Radio DJs, Event DJs
Website for Submissions:
https://crateconnect.com/

10. IDJPool

Popular Genres: Top 40, Hip-hop, Dance, House, R&B
Types of DJs: Radio DJs, Club DJs, Mobile DJs
Website for Submissions:
https://www.idjpool.com/

11. MP3Waxx

Popular Genres: Hip-hop, R&B, Reggae, EDM, Pop
Types of DJs: Club DJs, Radio DJs, Event DJs
Website for Submissions:
https://mp3waxx.com/

12. Promo Only

Popular Genres: Top 40, Urban, Dance, Country, Rock
Types of DJs: Radio DJs, Club DJs, Mobile DJs
Website for Submissions
https://promoonly.com/

13. Heavy Hits

Popular Genres: Hip-hop, EDM, Latin, Pop, Reggae
Types of DJs: Club DJs, Radio DJs, Event DJs
Website for Submissions
https://heavyhits.com/

14. 8th Wonder Promotions

Popular Genres: Hip-hop, R&B, Reggae, Dance, Pop
Types of DJs: Club DJs, Radio DJs, Mobile DJs
Website for Submissions:
https://www.8thwonderpromos.com/

15. Crate Gang

Popular Genres: Hip-hop, R&B, EDM, Reggae, Top 40
Types of DJs: Club DJs, Radio DJs, Event DJs
Website for Submissions:
https://www.crategang.com/

21. Serato Whitelabel.net

Popular Genres: Hip-hop, EDM, House, R&B, Pop
Types of DJs: Club DJs, Radio DJs, Event DJs
Website for Submissions:
https://serato.com/whitelabel

22. SmashVision

Popular Genres: Hip-hop, R&B, EDM, Latin, Pop
Types of DJs: Video DJs, Club DJs, Event DJs. SmashVision has a focus on music videos. Therefore, they would be great if you want to run a YouTube channel as a DJ.
Website for Submissions:
https://smashvision.com/

25. ZipDJ

Popular Genres: House, EDM, Hip-hop, Pop, Latin
Types of DJs: Club DJs, Radio DJs, Event DJs
Website for Submissions:
https://www.zipdj.com/contact-us/

Chapter 8: Blogging

In this chapter we are going to talk about blogging. This will include why we should keep a blog, the pros and cons of keeping a blog, thoughts and considerations, the different elements of a post and what you need to do in order to be a success. We are starting with a look at the pros and cons of blogging and why you need to be consistent if you keep a blog.

To Blog, Or Not to Blog? That is the Question

The reason I used this title to the chapter is not because I used to live in the town where William Shakespeare was born and raised. Rather, the point of this chapter is to address the pros and cons and give you enough information going forward to decide whether or not blogging is something you can do.

We look at both the pros and the cons of blogging and discuss how you can blog from a musical viewpoint. So, let's firstly take a look at the pros...

Multiple Streams of Passive Income

I have seen YouTube videos that suggest that keeping
a YouTube channel can be more lucrative than blogging. I actually do both. There are many ways

to monetize both your YouTube channel and your blog.

For instance, a YouTube channel can attract advertising revenue. You can also sell merch on YouTube. However, you can do both of these things with a blog too.

Here are a few more ideas that can be fodder for both your YouTube channel and your blog.

- Affiliate marketing
- Sell digital products that are either created by you, or for you
- Create webinars
- As a musician, you can add tuitional videos
- Sell merchandise directly from your site with Woocommerce.
- Sell advertising space
- Collect emails for an e-course

A WordPress.org Blog Gives You Full Control

Another major factor in favour of blogging is that you can customise it to anything you like. You have full, 100% control over your blog. There are a multitude of blog themes on the internet. Therefore, you should be able to find something that is just what you want. You can expect to pay anywhere from $10 to $100 for a WordPress theme.

The current theme at Krannaken.com was installed by David Risley of the Blog Marketing Academy. David did some work on the blog and gave it a bit of a facelift from what it used to be. You can find BMA at https://blogmarketingacademy.com/

Minimal Expenditure

If you want to blog on WordPress, you have minimal expenditure for your domain and hosting. You can expect a domain to cost no more than $15 (often much less) and your hosting would cost around $3-$5 per month for shared hosting. This latter figure is monthly, whereas the cost for your domain is an annual payment.

Since the last edition of this book, I have switched to a managed web hosting platform that brings in more traffic. This is quite a bit more expensive, but I believe it is worth my time and money.

You Will Be Considered as an Expert

If you have sufficient knowledge and experience to blog about your subject, you are considered an expert. Whether or not you currently are an expert in your subject is irrelevant. In any case, your research will build your knowledge in your area.

Therefore, you will soon become an expert and your knowledge will also build your confidence.

The benefit of being an expert is that you will become a go-to person for your readers. If they need advice, they will ask you for your opinion. This means that you can also promote products to them that you recommend. You can sell affiliate products and your readers will be happy to pay.

During your research, you will be researching different aspects of your industry. Research builds knowledge, and knowledge builds expertise. Your expertise will make you a more valuable person to your readers. Therefore, you will be paid more in return.

It is like reading a book and being a lifelong student. Books make knowledge, knowledge makes value and value makes expertise. Expertise will make you more sought after and this in turn means that you can expect a greater financial income.

Ultimate Flexibility Over Your Time

You will find that you can work on your own terms. If you have to take time out during the day, you can do what you have to do and blog in the evening. This means that you can get your kids to school and not worry about what time you are going to turn up for work.

However, you have to be careful that you are not too laid back about this. Remember that your blog will not write and promote itself. You have to work towards your business when you can and be careful that you are spending sufficient time with it.

For instance, if you are working on your blog full-time, you can expect to be spending at least 20 hours per week on blogging and blogging-related activities.

If you feel tired in the mornings, take a nap – especially if you need to do a video for your blog. On our site at Krannaken.com, we use video.

I have now switched to making YouTube videos with an artificially intelligent voiceover. It sounds great. I can use my own expression and convey it to the AI. The AI actually sounds very realistic and I've had some excellent success with it. At the time of writing this post, I have 614 subscribers on YouTube.

Since I have finished my University education, I now work full-time on my business. I tend to do the blogging and YouTube videos well in advance and make them the first thing I do in the week. Left over time is spent on further activities such as working on the next issue of The Complete Guide to Music Marketing.

As you will see if you go to Krannaken.com, I am passionate about my subject. You can tell that immediately – as soon as you see the website.
However, I am often tired in the mornings. I feel great when I make blog content. I feel like I am making a real difference to someone's life and someone's music. Therefore, I am going to keep at it.

Blogging is Great For SEO

Search engines such as Google love fresh content. Therefore, they rank websites that offer fresh content much higher than sites that never, or rarely, have a change of content. An active blog is being updated sometimes on a daily basis so the search engines will look at each page and rank them accordingly. If you do a Google search for a particular subject, it will normally always deliver blog posts at the top of the list.

Therefore, it is great to rank for particular search terms. Some of the best search terms to rank for are geographic-conscious. For instance, a blog that ranks for "rock bands in Chigwell, Essex" will attract a lot of attention. Maybe a venue is looking to hire a band that plays rock music in Chigwell. That means your post will be prominent in search results for people searching those search terms.

Selling Digital Products

As electronic musicians, you can sell digital products that you design especially for music artists. These could include sample packs, templates, preset packs or video courses. Such products can be downloaded quickly and easily from a website that uses WooCommerce. Therefore, this means that once I put the products on the website, they sell and distribute themselves. Sure enough, I have to do a little promotion of the products in my blog, but that is all I need to do. Sometimes, I add products to my blog posts, but that is all.

The Cons of Blogging

Just as there are some distinct positive points in blogging, there are also several negative points. These include…

It is Time Consuming

When you consider what a blogger does, it is not all about typing blog posts. In fact, typing blog posts takes less time than the rest of the blogger's responsibilities. Much more time is spent doing things like researching the subject and promoting the blog posts. It takes time to build connections, build your community and your tribe. You also have to factor in the creation of digital products that you are either selling or giving away free on your website.

It is Easy to be Too Flexible

As I have already said, flexibility can be unproductive if you are too laid back. This leads to neglect and the formation of poor habits. This is a poor work ethic and it is vital that you set sufficient time aside for blogging. If you want to blog full-time, you need to set at least 20 hours a week for blogging-related activities.

If Writing is Not Your Thing…

If you are not confident in your ability to write well, blogging probably isn't your thing. Ask yourself: "Would I rather write blog posts?", or "Am I better at making videos?". If the latter is true, maybe you should consider setting up and running a YouTube channel. I have written a part of this book on social media and that includes working with your own YouTube channel.

You May Need Some Technical Knowledge

This is not essential as you can find the right advice by contacting a technical specialist such as your hosting provider. However, if you want to work with your website without any fuss and without technical headaches, it may be worth your time to learn more about technical aspects of running a website..

I have to hold my hands up and say, "I am not a technical Wizard". If I need to find out how to do something I will either search for YouTube videos or Google it and see what results I get from a Google search. If I am still unable to find what I am looking for, I will search for a technical support email, submit a ticket or find a chat facility. Using these facilities gives you an almost immediate answer. The vast majority of the time, these people have found exactly what I need – and sometimes they even do the task themselves.

Negative Feedback From People Who Seem to Hate You

There will always be people who appear to hate you. It is an unfortunate part of sharing your thoughts and ideas in your digital products.

Krannaken TV is doing really well now, having 614 subscribers at the time of writing. By the time you are reading this, hopefully there will be a few more. The channel is getting some great feedback. You have to tell yourself that if you put your time and hard work into creating a video, it is worth sharing with the world. Feedback has come from various different people and I am much happier now that I am actually helping people.

You, too, could receive negative feedback at first. However, my advice to you is that you should not let this stop you from doing what you think you should be doing. If you have a passion for a subject, you need to share that passion with the world.

Wealth Does Not Come Overnight

If you want to make money from your blog, you are going to have to be consistent, yet patient. Patience is key. It may take some time to build your blog and have it looking great. My website looks great, but I am not getting a lot of traffic. I keep looking at my analytics and it doesn't seem to go very far, very quickly. However, I am building my community and my YouTube channel is an integral part of that.

My advice to you is to never lose sight of your goal. Be consistent. If you say you are going to blog five times a week, keep at it.

Considerations For Your Blog

The first considerations for your blog are your domain and hosting. You may be tempted to call it, yourname.com. For instance, our website is Krannaken.com. Krannaken is our artist name as musicians. Therefore, we are happy to call it that. As a musician, you are going to want people to listen to your music based on your artist name. If someone searched davidverney.com, they would find that the domain is for sale for a couple of thousand dollars. Don't ask me why that is. I don't know, but Krannaken.com has been with me for a while now and since Everhald came on board, our exposure as musical artists has grown. We will use each other as musical sounding boards and part of the reason why my music has improved so much is because I have had expert advice from Everhald, my University mentors and the people at Sonic Academy.

There are several good hosting companies. Personally, I favour Namecheap. They have great basic hosting. On this platform, I have been able to build a beautiful website and I am very passionate about it.

In 2024, I switched from Namecheap to Siteground. The reason for this was because managed hosting can generate much more traffic.

After your domain and hosting are complete, you will need to look at email marketing. Which autoresponder are you going to use. There are some good services with a free basic plan. Perhaps the most notable of these is MailChimp. There are also some premium services who offer an excellent and professional service such as GetResponse and Aweber.

For Krannaken.com, we have used SendFox. The deal there is a limit of 5,000 for a one-off payment of $49. Once I reach that 5,000 mark, I need to spend $10 per 1,000 so when I reach 10,000 subscribers, I will have paid $99. However, I now use ConvertKit and get a typical open-rate of 33%.

Then, you have to find the right visuals and image sources. I currently use Canva for everything. They have an amazing platform where I can get all of the assets I need. They will provide me with images and videos, as well as allow me to edit them. I bought an annual subscription for something like $79. I believe it is well worth that price.

Elements of Your Blog

Your website should include an "About" page, where you let people know why they should bother with your blog. Therefore, you need to include your unique selling proposition. What is different about your website that is not found anywhere else? At Krannaken.com, you can find a lot about music marketing strategies. You don't get this everywhere and there is a definite need for my content..

Another element you need to consider is your portfolio. Are you going to upload your best work to your website? You can host both videos and audios on your website. Or, you can embed videos and audios on your website from sites such as YouTube, Spotify or SoundCloud. Using the latter method doesn't take up space on your hosting so may be a better option. However, embedding music and videos means that people can click away from your website to go to SoundCloud, YouTube or Spotify without a second's thought.

If you wish your blog visitors to contact you, you will need to include your contact details. Either that, or include Contact Form 7 (a plugin found on your WordPress.org plugins tab). Contact Form 7 does what it says on the tin. It allows visitors to email you with questions or concerns. If they wish to offer you a contract to do some musical work for them, this is often the first point of contact.

There used to be a page for our music at Krannaken.com. However, now I focus on helping other artists before I work on any music that we may have put together. In any case, you can still find our music on YouTube.

If you want people to form some sort of familiarity with your music, it is a great idea to include a "Music" page on your website.

Merchandise is another part of your business that you should include on your website. As I mentioned before, merchandise or "merch" (as it has been shortened to) is promotional products that pay you to advertise your music. How would you like to be paid with a nice profit for someone to wear a T-shirt with your band name on the front. That is what merchandising is all about.

If you really want people to share your content, you need to include social sharing features. Think of all the different social media sites. Which ones do you want to work with most? For us, we share more content on Facebook, LinkedIn and YouTube than anywhere else. Other sites you might want to include sharing features for are Twitter and Instagram. If you want to appeal to people of a certain profession, LinkedIn is good. If you want to type out a quick question, lyric or recommendation, Twitter can be useful. We use Twitter Better Tweet to Click plugin which our website visitors can click to mention a blog post, etc, on their Twitter accounts.

Writing a Blog Post

Your blog is the most powerful text post you can type. It can reach more people, affect more lives and generate the most income for you. This is because it is constantly being updated and Google loves fresh content. Not only that, you also share more blog content than you do anything else. You don't promote your affiliate links everywhere directly because that is being spammy.

It appears to me that most people are unclear of the definition of the term "spam". Spam is basically links to websites and web pages that have nothing to do with the content being shared in the blog post, post thread or wherever you are pasting links. If you want to avoid being spammy, you must keep to the subject of the thread. What are the other people talking about? How can you help other people to find the right information they require? It is these questions that you need to post about.

A good blog needs the following elements...

Eye Catching and Enticing Headline

When writing my headlines for Krannaken.com, I always use Coschedule's Headline Analysis tool. This gives my headline a score between 0 and 100. I am normally happy with anything over 70. The good thing about Coschedule's tool https://coschedule.com/headline-analyzer is that it shows you the words which score something. There are four categories of words that it looks for. These are common, uncommon, emotional and powerful words. If you can build your headlines with a good number of all of these elements, you can get a great headline that people will click on to learn more and read your blog post. The Coschedule tool also measures the number of characters and words in your title. Around 50 to 60 characters is perfect and anywhere between 8 and 10 words is what the tool is looking for.

Introductory Paragraph

Your introductory paragraph has to lead people into the main body of the post. You should include why people need to read your post. What subjects or issues are you going to cover? How are you going to help people to improve whatever you are helping them to improve? Are you serious, joking or somewhere in the middle? Is your post supposed to excite people and make them feel a sense of fun?

You also need to include your main keyword in the opening paragraph. In case you are unfamiliar with the word "keyword", it is often a group of words that mean something. This can be something like "music marketing strategies" or "how to make music with. FL Studio". What would the people who appreciate your post, type into Google?

Pinnable Images

One thing you could put into your blog posts is a pinnable image with something akin to the headline in clear and readable text on the front. In my experience, pinners often add pins that are difficult to read. You should consider how easy it is for your pins to be read. If they are clear and the copy is good, you should be able to get repins and shares of your pinnable images. However, I always add a caption that reads something to the effect of "Please pin this image to relevant Pinterest boards. Thank you". This way people are more likely to pin your image.

To create your pins, I want to recommend a couple of different tools. These are Canva and RelayThat.

These are competitors. Most people use Canva, although I have a lifetime membership with RelayThat so I often use that instead.

You can find Canva here - https://www.canva.com/
You can find RelayThat here - https://relaythat.com/

How to Write the Main Body of Your Blog Post

You should write the main body of your blog post in a common-sense way that means something to you. What would you expect the order to be? If it is a list post, start with the least significant part of the list and work your way down to number one where you have the ultimate part of your list. For instance, if you were writing the top ten list of guitars, you would start with the cheaper, no-frills entry and work your way to the most expensive and best guitar that you know of.

Similarly, if you are writing about a process, you would obviously start at the very beginning of the process and write about each step of the process in the order it is implemented.

Affiliate Banners

If you are appealing to a certain group of people with your blog post, you should include affiliate banners so that you can monetize your post.

With affiliate marketing, you refer people to a product or website where they can purchase products and services. When people purchase a product after being directed from your website, you make a commission. This can be any amount at all.

On Krannaken.com, I work with Loopmasters, LoopCloud and Plugin Boutique. These are all sister-companies and all provide digital products for musicians. Digital products pay the best money. However, this is not the reason I use these programs. My biggest reason for using these programs is because they offer the best customer experience. I want my readers to appreciate these opportunities to purchase from the best music software providers.

Better Click to Tweet

Better Click to Tweet is a plugin that enables bloggers to write an enticing sentence in the tweet box and have blog visitors click to tweet. All it takes is two clicks and they have left, what is in essence, an endorsement on their Twitter feed.

Closing with a Call to Action (CTA)

Every blog post should have a call to action. It could be something as simple as leaving a comment on the blog, requesting an email address, purchasing a product or service mentioned in the blog post, or subscribing to your blog feed. However, you must make it as easy as possible for your readers to make the decision to carry out your request. If you want people to subscribe to either your newsletter or your blog feed, you should link to your blog feed from the sentence that makes the request.

Another thing that I probably should have pointed out earlier in this chapter is SEO. With the right keywords, you can generate as much traffic as you need. Most of the traffic on Krannaken.com comes from Google and I love using a site called KeySearch.co to get tonnes of the best keywords.

Keeping a Consistent Schedule

The actual writing of your blog posts take up a small part of your duties. Some bloggers talk about the 80/20 rule. This rule has been applied to many different aspects of running a business. However, when it comes to blogging, the 80/20 rule means 80% of your time is spent in promoting your blog post, as opposed to 20% of your time in which you write your posts. Therefore, blogging on a daily basis is difficult for most people. You either end up writing a better blog post with a poorer promotion campaign or you write a poorer blog post with a better promotion campaign. Either way, it doesn't really work. You need to focus on one or another. However, if you have fewer blog posts, you don't have as many pieces of content to attract more attention. Therefore, it is a better idea to blog less often.

I have taken to writing my blog posts just three days per week now and I have them written three weeks in advance. Therefore, I have more time for all the promotion.

I Just Hit Publish...What Do I Do Now?

There are a lot of ways to get traffic to a website. We are going to look at some of the best. By the best, I mean the traffic generation strategies that will bring you the most attention from the right target market.

Firstly, I will give you the methods that I use to drive traffic. However, I will talk about other website traffic generation strategies too.

The site that I use mostly for my traffic is Pinterest. However, I use a third-party plugin for Pinterest: Tailwind.

Tailwind allows me to post content to my tribes who share my content on their Pinterest boards. Some of these are group boards. This means that when people post to them, they will in-turn, be sharing their images with entire groups of people with a massive following.

Tailwind also schedules my content at optimum times when more people are viewing them on Pinterest at peak times of the day. This boosts my chances of finding successful blog traffic with each pin.

Email Marketing

It is also vital that you send your emails to your list at the best times for them. What time of day do you normally post at? Does this fit in with your list members. This is a big plus point for Aweber. They allow you to publish content at times of your list location. Therefore, you can set it to publish at 9.30am for your list and your list will receive your emails at 9.39am in their own local times.

If people missed your initial email, it is a good idea to send out another email so that the people who missed the first email can read the second email. That way, you are maximising open-rates and click through-rates.

Another good idea for your email marketing is to add a social share button within the email itself. Your list members will then be able to share your email to their Facebook, Twitter or whatever you choose.

In every email you send out, no matter who it is to, you should add your website to your signature. You can set it so that it appears automatically. Furthermore, it does not matter whether your emails are private or public, or whatever else. It is always a good idea to show people your website in your email signature.

Blogging Communities

Blog syndicate and aggregate sites are also worth posting your latest blog post to. These help by sharing your content with group members. There are some really big sites like Reddit and some more specialised to the "Making Money Online" niche. These latter includes sites like Kingged and BizSugar. For a full rundown of these sites, please see Chapter 13: Websites For Musicians.

Both Question and Answer Sites (often abbreviated to Q&A Sites) and forums offer you the opportunity to share your knowledge. As a musician, you can share your blog posts if they help other people. If you have the answers to their questions, it is great if you can show people how to solve whatever issue the thread is about.

Again, for a full list of these sites, please see Chapter 13. I am only going to list sites that are relevant to you as a musician, music producer or music industry professional.

It is a fantastic idea to create a secret group on Facebook that is known as an Inner Circle. This group is made up of people who you know will be able to help you. If it comes to sharing content, sharing your blog posts, or latest tracks, releases, etc, you can count on your Inner Circle to post your content to their social channels.

You also need to share your own social profiles. This includes Facebook, Twitter, LinkedIn, Google Plus, Tumblr, Pinterest and Instagram. Read more about these sites in Section Seven of this book.

Chapter 9: Artificial Intelligence

AI offers a wide variety of tools and services that can substantially benefit musicians, music artists, and composers.

Music Composition and Songwriting

AIVA (Artificial Intelligence Virtual Artist)

Features: AIVA is capable of composing classical-based music. Therefore, it is particularly good if you wish to create cinematic or any of the subgenres of classical music.

It also has the ability to compose music for film scores, video games, and commercials.

AIVA offers pre-set styles and allows for some customisation.

Pros: Plus points for AIVA include its high-quality compositions that are suitable for professional use. It is customisable. Therefore, it fits various project needs. You can also generate sheet music with these advanced features

Cons: On the not-so-great side, AIVA is more suitable for classical and cinematic music. Therefore, there are limited genres. If you wish to make something different, you are better to go with another option.

It also requires some musical knowledge to maximise its potential. Whether this could be called a negative point, would be controversial. If it requires some prior knowledge, it would also require some skill. Therefore, there is a learning curve to it and you are learning all the time as you use it.

Use for Music Artists: As already mentioned, AIVA is great for composers needing orchestral or cinematic scores.

Website: https://www.aiva.ai/

Soundraw

Features: Soundraw offers AI-generated music that can be customised by duration of the track, mood, genre, theme and also whether you want a slow, moderate or fast tempo.

There is also integration with video editing software so that film productions of any genre can be created quickly and easily. This can include music videos.

Pros: There is fast generation of customizable tracks. All tracks are without copyright issues and it is easy to integrate Soundraw with other tools.

Cons: The music that can be created with Soundraw is limited to basic customization. Therefore, it may not suit all advanced needs.

Finally, on the downside, Soundraw requires a subscription for full access. They really need to monetize the platform somewhere and this is done through these premium subscriptions.

Use for Music Artists: Soundraw is a suitable tool for content creators needing background music for various media.

Website: https://soundraw.io/

Amadeus Code

Features: Amadeus features an AI-driven songwriting assistant. It can generate new melodies based on user inputs and preferences. You can also integrate Amadeus with other music production software.

Pros: Amadeus provides creative inspiration and new melody ideas.

It is also surprisingly easy to use with existing workflows. I say this because any app that calls itself "code" sounds like a technical nightmare. However, that is not how it is with Amadeus.

Cons: Amadeus is limited to melody generation and not full compositions.

It also requires additional tools for full song production.

Use for Music Artists: Amadeus is ideal for songwriters needing help with melody creation.

Website: https://amadeuscode.com/ Amadeus Code is available on the Apple App Store.

Humtap

Features: Users of Humtap can simply hum a tune, and the AI creates a full instrumental track. Therefore, it is accessible to everyone. Furthermore, it also boasts a simple interface with instant results.

Pros: Humtap offers a quick and intuitive way to capture musical ideas. Therefore, there is no need for extensive musical knowledge.

Cons: There is limited control over the final arrangement. It may be unsuitable for artists who like to get involved with the arrangement of the entire track.

There is also basic functionality. This makes it more suitable for idea generation than finishing, arranging and polishing the entire track.

Use for Music Artists: Humtap is useful for capturing spontaneous musical ideas and developing them further.

Website: https://www.humtap.com/ Humtap is available on the Apple App Store

Orb Composer 3

Features: Orb Composer 3 is a comprehensive AI composition software package for various music genres. It also offers deep customisation options for harmony, melody, and rhythm, as well as integration with major DAWs (Digital Audio Workstations).

Pros: On the plus side, Orb Composer 3 incorporates a high level of customisation and control. It is suitable for professional composers and producers and also supports complex compositions.

Cons: Orb Composer 3 has a steeper learning curve. Therefore, it can be difficult to use and is not very user-friendly. There is also a higher cost compared to simpler apps.

Use for Music Artists: Overall, Orb Composer offers an excellent option for professional composers needing detailed and complex arrangements.

Website: https://www.orbplugins.com/

Ecrett Music

Features: Ecrett offers AI-generated music for videos and games. As it's AI, it provides an easier way to compose music for games and videos that you can monetize and create a profit from.

It is also customizable by scene, mood, and genre.

Pros: Ecrett is easy to use with specific project templates, and provides a fast workflow with professional generation of tailored music.

Cons: There are limits to preset customization options. Therefore, you don't have full control over the sound and the sound quality.

Ecrett also requires a subscription for full access.

Use for Music Artists: Overall, Ecrett is great for content creators needing quick and tailored background music.

Website: https://ecrettmusic.com/

Lyric Writing

LyricStudio

Features: LyricStudio provides real-time lyric suggestions and inspiration. All music is customisable to match different styles and genres.

Pros: LyricStudio boasts a user-friendly interface. It also helps the artist to overcome writer's block because it offers fresh ideas to work with..

Cons: Main disadvantages of using LyricStudio are that it requires a subscription for full features. It is also limited to lyric writing. There is no melody or music generation.

Use for Music Artists: LyricStudio is ideal for generating new lyric ideas and enhancing creativity.

Website: https://lyricstudio.net/

MasterWriter

Features: MasterWriter has a comprehensive suite of tools for songwriters, including a rhyming dictionary, thesaurus, and phrase ideas. It offers a database of cultural references and phrases.

Pros: MasterWriter enhances lyrics with richer vocabulary and references. It is user-friendly and has an organised interface.

Cons: On the negative side, MasterWriter can be overwhelming with the amount of information available.

Use for Music Artists: Overall, MasterWriter is ideal for enhancing lyrics with richer vocabulary and cultural references.

Website: https://masterwriter.com/

DeepBeat

Features: Specifically, DeepBeat is designed for generating rap lyrics. It uses deep learning to understand and generate rhyme patterns.

Pros: DeepBeat generates and refines rap lyrics quickly.

Cons: It is specifically focused on rap and hip-hop genres. This may be a negative point for those of you who don't make music that falls within the rap and hip-hop genre or subgenres.

The interface is simple and it has fewer customisation options. For some this will be a plus point. However, if you want full control over everything, you are better to pick another option.

Use for Music Artists: DeepBeat is perfect for rappers looking to generate and refine lyrics quickly.

Website: https://deepbeat.org/

These Lyrics Do Not Exist

Features: With its confusing name These Lyrics Do Not Exist generates complete lyrics based on user-selected themes and genres. It is also free to use.

Pros: These Lyrics Do Not Exist offers quick lyric drafts and inspiration for various themes. It also has a simple and accessible interface.

Cons: Unfortunately, the lyrics that are generated can sometimes be generic and lack depth. There is also limited customization and user input.

Use for Music Artists: These Lyrics Do Not Exist is useful for quick lyric drafts and thematic inspiration.

Website: https://theselyricsdonotexist.com/

Song Lyrics Generator by BoredHumans

Features: Song Lyrics Generator is simple and easy to use. It also offers free access.

Pros: Song Lyrics Generator provides basic functionality for quick idea generation and it is accessible for beginners.

Cons: Its basic functionality with limited customization make it less appealing and the lyrics it generates can also be repetitive and less original.

Use for Music Artists: Song Lyrics Generator is good for brainstorming and quick idea generation.

Website: https://boredhumans.com/song_lyrics_generator.php

LyricFind

Features: LyricFind has an extensive database of lyrics for reference and inspiration. It also provides tools for creating and organising lyrics.

Pros: LyricFind is useful for finding musical inspiration and referencing existing lyrics. It also has a comprehensive lyric search tool.

Cons: This software is not specifically an AI lyric generator, but instead it is more of a search and reference tool.

Use for Music Artists: LyricFind is ideal for finding inspiration and referencing existing lyrics.

Website: https://www.lyricfind.com/

Music Production

Mixing and Mastering

LANDR

Features: LANDR is an artificially intelligent mastering tool with genre-specific algorithms. It offers instant mastering previews, a cloud-based platform with collaboration tools and distribution services for releasing music.

It's unique selling points include being a quick and easy to use way to master music that provides high-quality results. It provides mixing as well as mastering services.

Pros: If the above insights into the great thing weren't enough to win you over, LANDR also provides a fast turnaround time, intuitive interface and has affordable subscription plans.

Cons: Believe it or not, there are some cons. These include the fact that it has limited customization compared to traditional mastering. It is also less suitable for complex or highly specialised tracks.

Use for Music Artists: LANDR is ideal for independent artists and producers looking for quick and affordable mastering solutions.

Website: https://www.landr.com/

eMastered

Features: eMastered offers AI-powered mastering with dynamic range control, customisable sound options and A/B comparison with original track.

It's unique selling points are that it offers a user friendly interface with real-time previews. It also offers mastering tailored to various different genres.

Pros: On the plus side, eMastered offers high-quality output. It is easy to use and it has very affordable one-time fees or subscription.

Cons: Unfortunately, eMastered has limited in-depth control for advanced users. There are also occasional issues with specific genres or complex tracks.

Use for Music Artists: eMastered is suitable for artists and producers seeking a quick and efficient mastering service.

Website: https://emastered.com/

iZotope Ozone

Features: Ozone offers an advanced mastering suite with AI-powered Master Assistant, a comprehensive set of mastering tools and presets and integration with DAWs.

It offers professional-grade mastering capabilities. It is also highly customisable with deep control over the process.

Pros: Ozone also offers extensive customization options and integration with other iZotope plugins.

Cons: Unfortunately, it has a steeper learning curve, and higher cost compared to simpler solutions.

Use for Music Artists: Ozone is best for professional producers and engineers seeking deep control over mastering.

Website:
https://www.izotope.com/en/products/ozone.html

AI Mastering

Features: AI Mastering is as the name suggests, AI-driven mastering. However, there is a significant focus on simplicity and speed.

AI Mastering offers a cloud-based service with instant previews and it supports multiple file formats.

AI Mastering's unique selling points include extremely fast processing as well as being simple and straightforward interface.

Pros: Plus points include a very quick turnaround. It is easy to use for beginners and it offers affordable pricing - at the time of writing, an unlimited mastering plan is available for free.

Cons: Negative points include limited customization options. Also, it may not handle complex tracks as well as more advanced tools.

Use for Music Artists: AI Mastering is ideal for quick, hassle-free mastering of demo tracks and releases.

Website: https://aimastering.com/

Aria Mastering

Features: Aria offers AI-driven mastering with analog processing emulation, customisable mastering preferences and multiple mastering versions for comparison.

The unique selling points include the combination of AI technology with analog mastering techniques. It also provides different mastering versions for better choice.

Pros: With high-quality, warm analog sound, user-friendliness and customization capabilities, together with affordable pricing options, Aria is a realistic option for many.

Cons: However, it is limited to mastering. There are no mixing features and it can be less intuitive for new users.

Use for Music Artists: Aria is perfect for artists seeking a warm, analog sound in their masters.

Website: https://ariamastering.com/

BandLab Mastering

Features: BandLab features AI-powered mastering with genre-specific settings, integration with the BandLab music creation platform. It is also a free service with unlimited use.

The unique selling points include the fact that it is completely free of charge. It also offers integration with a full music production platform.

Pros: Plus points include the free price point as well as unlimited mastering, easiness of use and its provision of good quality results.

Cons: Being free you would expect poorer quality and a lack of options. However, BandLab comes with all this and it's still free. Maybe the fact that it is free is a red flag for some.

Use for Music Artists: BandLab is Ideal for beginners and hobbyists needing a free mastering solution.

Website: https://www.bandlab.com/mastering

Sound Design

Please also see the pages about music composition and songwriting which was included earlier in this chapter.

Magenta Studio

Features: Magenta offers music production, harmony, and rhythm design with Integration with Ableton Live.

The unique selling points include being open-source and, therefore, free of charge. However, tools for deep customisation are also included. There is also a focus on creative exploration.

Pros: Being open-source, Magenta is a free option, but also a highly customisable option that supports creative and experimental sound design.

Cons: Magenta requires knowledge of Ableton Live for full functionality. This makes it not as user-friendly for beginners.

Use for Music Artists: With experimental sound design and music creation, Magenta offers a good option for Ableton Live users.

Website:
https://magenta.tensorflow.org/studio/ableton-live

Boomy

Features: Boomy features AI-generated music tracks, customizable genre, mood, and instrumentation.

Unique selling points include its Ease of use and quick music creation. It is also suitable for non-musicians.

Pros: Plus points include a user-friendly interface, and the ability to generate royalty-free music.

Cons: Boomy has limited control over fine details and a subscription is also required for full access. It is easy to take it for granted if you are producing music on such a mass scale.

Use for Music Artists: Great for creating music tracks that are suitable for both personal and commercial use.

Website: https://boomy.com/

Sononym

Features: Sononym features AI-driven sample search and organisation. It also analyses and categorises samples based on sound characteristics. These features would make it a direct competitor of LoopCloud.

The unique selling points include advanced sample analysis and management features and assistance in discovering new and relevant samples.

Pros: Sononym saves time in searching for great samples. It also has an intuitive interface.

Cons: It is limited to sample management and requires a large sample library for best results.

Use for Music Artists: Sononym is useful for organising and discovering samples for music production.

Website: https://www.sononym.net/

Personalised Learning

Music Education

Yousician

Features: Yousician provides interactive lessons for guitar, piano, bass, ukulele, and singing. It also provides real-time feedback on accuracy and timing. There is an extensive library of songs and exercises that is included in the app.

Perhaps Yousician's unique selling point is its gamified learning experience with real-time feedback.

Pros: Yousician is fun, engaging, and suitable for all skill levels. It also offers a structured learning path.

Cons: If you hope to use Yousician, you will be required to have a subscription. This will give you full access. There is also limited customization for advanced players.

Use for Music Artists: Yousician is ideal for both beginners and intermediate players looking for structured practice.

Website: https://www.yousician.com/

Simply Piano by JoyTunes

Features: Simply Piano, as the name suggests, provides step-by-step piano lessons with interactive feedback, a large library of songs across various genres and it is suitable for all ages and skill levels.

Simply Piano's unique selling point is that it provides simplified piano learning with a user-friendly interface.

Pros: Simply Piano is easy to follow and very beginner-friendly. It also racks progress and adjusts difficulty accordingly.

Cons: Unfortunately, there is limited advanced content. It also requires a subscription for full access.

Use for Music Artists: Simply Piano is perfect for beginners wanting to learn piano at their own pace.

Website: https://www.joytunes.com/apps/simply-piano/

SmartMusic

Features: SmartMusic provides interactive practice with immediate feedback, a large library of exercises and sheet music. It can also be integrated with music education curriculums.

The unique selling point is that it is a comprehensive tool for both individual practice and classroom use.

Pros: SmartMusic is suitable for various instruments and skill levels. It also provides you with detailed performance reports.

Cons: SmartMusic requires users to have a subscription. The interface is also too complex for beginners.

Use for Music Artists: SmartMusic is ideal for students and educators looking for a structured practice environment.

Website: https://www.smartmusic.com/

Moosiko

Features: Moosiko offers a guitar practice tool with personalised learning paths. It tracks progress and provides feedback. There is also a library of songs and exercises that are tailored to user's level.

The unique selling point is that Moosiko is focused on personalised learning for guitarists.

Pros: Moosiko offers customisable practice sessions, with encouragement and consistent practice habits.

Cons: Unfortunately Moosiko is limited to guitar. A subscription is also required for full access.

Use for Music Artists: Moosiko is great for guitarists seeking a personalised practice routine.

Website: https://www.moosiko.com/

Melodics

Features: Melodics features interactive lessons for MIDI keyboards, pad controllers, and electronic drums. It provides real-time feedback and progress tracking with a wide range of genres and styles.

The unique selling point is that it specialises in electronic music instruments.

Pros: On the plus side, it is suitable for both beginners and advanced users. There is also an engaging interface with a focus on modern music styles.

Cons: Melodics is limited to electronic instruments. A subscription is also required if the user wants access to all of the content.

Use for Music Artists: Melodics is ideal for electronic musicians and producers looking to improve their skills.

Website: https://melodics.com/

PlayScore 2

Features: PlayScore 2 uses AI to read sheet music and play it back. It can create MIDI files from scanned sheet music and it allows for tempo adjustments and practice loops.

The unique selling point is that it turns sheet music into playable audio for practice.

Pros: PlayScore 2 supports various music formats. It is useful for learning new pieces.

Cons: The cons include the requirement of high-quality scans for best results. A subscription is also needed for full features.

Use for Music Artists: PlayScore 2 is great for musicians who want to hear and practice along with their sheet music.

Website: https://www.playscore.co/

MyEarTraining

Features: As the name suggests, MyEarTraining provides ear training exercises for intervals, chords, scales, and rhythms. It also offers customisable practice sessions, it tracks progress and adapts to user's skill level.

MyEarTraining's unique selling point is that it offers a comprehensive ear training tool with AI adaptation.

Pros: MyEarTraining is suitable for all skill levels and it has extensive customization options.

Cons: Unfortunately, the interface may be complex for some users. Again, a subscription is also required for advanced features.

Use for Music Artists: MyEarTraining is ideal for musicians looking to improve their ear training and music theory skills.

Website: https://www.myeartraining.net/

Chordify

Features: Chordify converts songs into chords for guitar, piano, and ukulele. It provides an interactive experience for the instrumentalist with tempo control and looping. There is also an extensive library of more than 36 million songs to choose from.

The unique selling point for Chordify includes the fact that it simplifies learning chords for popular songs.

Pros: Chordify provides user-friendly and quick chord identification. It also supports multiple instruments.

Cons: Chordify is limited to chord identification. A subscription is also required for full access.

Use for Music Artists: Chordify is perfect for musicians wanting to quickly learn and play chords of their favorite songs.

Website: https://chordify.net/

Music Analysis and Insights

Music Theory Analysis

Hookpad

Features: Hookpad features an interactive music theory sketchpad. It analyses chord progressions and melodies and offers built-in music theory guides.

The main unique selling point is that it has a user-friendly interface for composing and analysing music. It also offers an extensive library of chords and scales.

Pros: Hookpad is a great educational tool for learning music theory. It also helps in creating and visualizing chord progressions.

Cons: Hookpad is limited to chord progressions and basic melody analysis. It also requires the user to have a subscription for maximum benefit.

Use for Music Artists: Hookpad is ideal for songwriters and musicians wanting to improve their understanding of music theory and create compositions.

Website: https://www.hooktheory.com/hookpad

Tonic AI

Features: Tonic AI offers AI-powered harmonic analysis with real-time chord recognition and progression analysis. It also integrates with all major DAWs.

The unique selling point is Tonic AI's provision of detailed harmonic analysis and chord recommendations as well as real-time analysis for live performances.

Pros: Tonic AI is highly accurate in chord recognition. It enhances music production with harmonic insights.

Cons: Primarily, Tonic AI is focused on harmonic analysis. You will also require a more advanced understanding of music production.

Use for Music Artists: Tonic AI is useful for producers and composers looking to enhance their harmonic understanding and create more complex compositions.

Website: https://www.tonic-ai.com/

Melodyne

Features: Melodyne offers pitch and time correction, detailed analytics for pitch, timing, and format. It also offers harmonic and melodic editing tools.

The unique selling point is that it offers the industry-standard for pitch correction and vocal editing. It also offers deep analysis and editing capabilities for audio tracks.

Pros: Melodyne offers highly accurate pitch and time correction, as well as advanced tools for harmonic and melodic analysis.

Cons: The cons include a steep learning curve for beginners and it is very expensive for the full feature set.

Use for Music Artists: Melodyne is ideal for professional music producers and sound engineers needing reliably precise pitch correction and detailed audio analysis.

Website: https://www.celemony.com/en/melodyne

Sibelius

Features: Sibelius is a music notation software with AI-driven analysis tools. It features harmonic, melodic, and rhythmic analysis and can be integrated with various DAWs and music software.

Sibelius is the Industry-standard for music notation and analysis and offers comprehensive tools for composition and arrangement.

Pros: Sibelius has powerful notation and analysis capabilities. It is also widely used in the music industry.

Cons: Sibelius is expensive for the full version and requires time to learn all features.

Use for Music Artists: Sibelius is ideal for composers, arrangers, and music educators who need advanced notation and analysis tools.

Website: https://www.avid.com/sibelius

Audience Analysis

Chartmetric

Features: Chartmetric Analyses streaming data, social media, playlist placements and provides insights into listener demographics and engagement. It also monitors chart performance and trends.

Chartmetric's main unique selling proposition is that it provides comprehensive analysis across multiple platforms.

Pros: In its favour, Chartmetric has in-depth data and insights. It also integrates various music data sources.

Cons: Chartmetric can be too complex for beginners. It also has a higher cost for advanced features.

Use for Music Artists: The main use for music artists is with its tracking performance and trends for music marketing and strategy.

Website: https://www.chartmetric.com/

Soundcharts

Features: Soundcharts features real-time monitoring of charts, playlists, and social media. It provides audience demographics and geographic data. Furthermore, it also provides competitive analysis and benchmarking.

The unique selling proposition is that it provides real-time data and competitive insights.

Pros: Soundcharts has a user-friendly interface, as well as real-time updates.

Cons: Soundcharts has limited free features. You will require a subscription for full access.

Use for Music Artists: Soundcharts shines through with its real-time monitoring and competitor analysis for music marketing.

Website: https://soundcharts.com/

SpotOnTrack

Features: Spot on Track is great for playlist tracking and analysis. It also provides Insights into playlist performance and reach and offers daily updates and historical data.

It's unique selling point lies in its focus on playlist performance.

Pros: The great things about SpotOnTrack include its detailed playlist analysis as well as easy-to-use interface.

Cons: Unfortunately, it is limited to playlist data so you wouldn't be able to track radio airplay, etc, with it. It is also subscription-based.

Use for Music Artists: SpotOnTrack comes into its own with monitoring and analysing playlist success.

Website: https://www.spotontrack.com/

Viberate

Features: Viberate tracks streaming, social media, and live performances. It also provides audience insights and engagement metrics and includes a database of artists, venues, and events.

Viberate is a comprehensive platform including live performance data.

Pros: Viberate provides a wide range of data sources. It is user friendly too.

Cons: Viberate has limited free features. It is also more focused on live performance data.

Use for Music Artists: The main use comes with its comprehensive artist and performance analysis.

Website: https://www.viberate.com/

Audience Republic

Features: Audience Republic has event and ticket sales analytics as well as audience segmentation and targeting. It includes integration with CRM and marketing tools.

The unique selling proposition for Audience Republic lies in its focus on events and ticket sales.

Pros: Audience Republic boasts detailed event data and strong CRM integration.

Cons: Primarily, Audience Republic is focused on events, not streaming. It is also subscription based.

Use for Music Artists: Its strengths lie in its analysing and optimising of event ticket sales and audience targeting.

Website: https://www.audiencerepublic.com/

Collaboration and Networking

Virtual Collaboration

Soundtrap by Spotify

Features: Soundtrap features an online DAW with real-time collaboration as well as built-in instruments, loops, and effects. It also integrates with Spotify for easy sharing.

It's unique selling proposition is in its seamless integration with Spotify. It is also a comprehensive DAW and comes complete with collaborative tools.

Pros: Soundtrap has a user-friendly interface, extensive library of sounds and loops. It also provides cross-platform access (web, iOS, Android).

Cons: Soundtrap requires a subscription for full features. It can also be resource-intensive on some devices.

Use for Music Artists: Soundtrap is great for collaborative music production and sharing projects with a wider audience.

Website: https://www.soundtrap.com/

BandLab

Features: Cloud-based DAW with real-time collaboration and social networking features for musicians. BandLab also provides integrated mastering tools.

The unique selling propositions include the fact that it is free to use with a rich feature set and also boasts a strong focus on social interaction and sharing.

Pros: BandLab provides easy collaboration with other musicians as well as access to a large community of artists and cross-platform compatibility (web, iOS, Android).

Cons: Limitations include few advanced features compared to professional DAWs. Some users may also find the social features distracting.

Use for Music Artists: BandLab is great for collaborative projects and connecting with other musicians.

Website: https://www.bandlab.com/

Splice

Features: Splice is a cloud-based collaboration and storage solution with an extensive library of samples and loops as well as project sharing and version control facilities.

Splice's unique selling propositions include its large and high-quality sample library as well as advanced collaboration and backup features.

Pros: On the plus side, Splice is easy to share and collaborate on projects. It integrates extremely well with major DAWs and it offers frequent updates and new content.

Cons: A subscription is required for full access to all of the features on Splice. It is also more focused on sample-based production.

Use for Music Artists: Splice is ideal for producers who are looking for high-quality samples and collaborative tools.

Website: https://splice.com/

Kompoz

Features: Kompoz is an online music collaboration platform that is community-driven with project-based collaboration. It also provides tools for organising and managing contributions.

The unique selling proposition lies in its focus on community collaboration and project management. Kompoz also supports a wide range of musical genres.

Pros: Users of Kompoz are encouraged to collaboration across different styles and locations around the world. There are tools included for managing complex projects. Kompoz also has a large and active user base.

Cons: Kompoz has limited DAW capabilities compared to other platforms. It also requires a paid subscription for premium features.

Use for Music Artists: Kompoz is best for collaborative projects involving multiple contributors.

Website: https://www.kompoz.com

Soundation

Features: Soundation features an online DAW with real-time collaboration, integrated instruments, effects, and loops. It is also known for its community and sharing features.

Soundation's leading USP is that it is accessible from any web browser on the planet. It also offers real-time collaboration with integrated chat.

Pros: There are no software installations required in order to get maximum benefit. It is also easy to use with a clean interface and there is a free tier available with essential features.

Cons: The advanced features on Soundation require a paid subscription. These are also limited compared to full desktop DAWs.

Use for Music Artists: Soundation is more suitable for quick, collaborative projects and beginners.

Website: https://soundation.com/

Music Remixes

LANDR Remix

Features: LANDR Remix offers an AI-driven remixing tool that allows users to upload their own tracks for remixing. It can remix music in a variety of styles and genres.

LANDR Remix offers an easy-to-use interface along with fast and automated remix generation.

Pros: LANDR Remix offers high-quality remixes that are generated quickly. It also has a very user-friendly platform and various style options.

Cons: Unfortunately, there are limited customisation features beyond preset styles and it requires a paid subscription for full access with the maximum benefits.

Use for Music Artists: LANDR Remix is ideal for DJs and producers looking for quick remix solutions. It should also be noted that LANDR have a name for high-quality products. Therefore, this would be a wise option.

Website: https://landr.com

Mixed In Key Mashup

Features: Mixed In Key Mashup features AI-assisted mashup creation. It also analyses key and tempo of tracks for seamless mixing.and provides suggestions for compatible tracks.

Mixed In Key Mashup's main unique selling points lie in its focus on harmonic mixing and its assistance in creating professional-sounding mashups.

Pros: Other pros include its targeted accuracy in key and tempo matching. It is also easy to create complex mashups.

Cons: Mixed In Key Mashup is limited to mashup creation rather than full remixes. It may also require some manual adjustment for perfect results.

Use for Music Artists: Mixed In Key Mashup is perfect for DJs looking to create harmonic mashups quickly.

Website: https://mixedinkey.com

Algoriddim djay

Features: Agoriddm djay features AI-powered DJ software as well as an automix AI to create seamless transitions and remixes. It also integrates with streaming services.

The main unique selling point for Algoriddm djay lies in its real-time remixing and DJing and advanced AI for live performance.

Pros: Algoriddm djay is a versatile tool for live DJ sets, high-quality automixing features and it offers integration with popular streaming services.

Cons: Algoriddm djay requires hardware (e.g., DJ controllers) for full functionality. A subscription model is also required for advanced features.

Use for Music Artists: Algoriddm djay is also suitable for live DJ performances and practice sessions.

Website: https://algoriddim.com

Music Distribution and Promotion

Algorithmic Playlists

Spotify

Features: Perhaps Spotify is your first consideration when you think of algorithmic playlists. These AI playlists include Discover Weekly as well as other personalised playlists based on listening habits. These other algorithmic playlists also include Release Radar for new music recommendations based on user preferences and Daily Mixes which are genre-based playlists created from user listening history.

Spotify's unique selling points include an extensive library with millions of tracks as well as highly accurate personalization algorithms.

Pros: Spotify offers consistently updated playlists, a high level of customization and an easy-to-use interface.

Cons: Spotify has to monetise the free membership plan with advertising. There are also some features such as audiobooks that are behind a paywall.

Use for Music Artists: Spotify comes into its own with its ability to introduce new music to users through it's algorithmic playlists. It is great for creating personalised music experiences.

Website: https://www.spotify.com

Apple Music

Features: Apple is great for its curated playlist, For You. This is based on user preferences.

There is also the New Music Mix which is a weekly updated playlist of new releases.

Chill Mix is yet another Apple algorithmic playlist. It offers a selection of relaxing tracks based on listening habits.

Apple's unique selling proposition lies in its deep integration with the Apple ecosystem as well as high-quality audio streaming.

Pros: Apple Music provides excellent sound quality, exclusive releases and content as well as seamless integration with Apple devices.

Cons: Limitations include the facts that it is less effective for discovering niche genres and there are higher subscription costs.

Use for Music Artists: Just as with Spotify, Apple is great if you are looking for new music and exclusive content. It also integrates music seamlessly across Apple devices.

Website: https://www.apple.com/apple-music/

Pandora

Features: Pandora offers its Music Genome Project. This is an algorithmic playlist creation based on song attributes. It also offers personalised stations that are created from user feedback (thumbs up/down).

Pandora Modes offers different listening modes for variety, discovery, and more.

Pandora also offers highly detailed music analysis for precise recommendations.

Pros: On the plus side, Pandora includes highly personalised stations, as well as easy feedback mechanism for better recommendations.

Cons: There is less international availability than its competitors. There is also a lot of advertising in the free version.

Use for Music Artists: Pandora is great for creating highly personalised radio stations. It is also great for discovering new music through detailed song analysis.

Website: https://www.pandora.com

YouTube Music

Features: Personalised mixes: created based on user watch and listen history.
YouTube also offers its Discover Mix which is a weekly updated playlist of new and trending music. There is also My Supermix which is a blend of user favorites and new recommendations.

YouTube Music's unique selling proposition is its integration with YouTube for music videos and live performances.

Pros: YouTube Music offers access to a vast library of music videos, as well as seamless integration with the YouTube video platform.

Cons: There is heavy advertising in the free version and a requirement for YouTube Premium if you would prefer an ad-free experience.

Use for Music Artists: Again, as with the other platforms, YouTube is great if you want to discover new music and watch high-quality music videos. It is also great for creating personalised playlists based on viewing and listening habits.

Website: https://music.youtube.com

Tidal

Features: Tidal has its My Mix: personalised playlists which are based on user listening habits. Other playlists include Tidal Rising which promotes new and emerging artists and further editorial playlists which are curated by Tidal's music experts.

Tidal's unique selling points include high-fidelity sound quality and Hi-Res audio, as well as exclusive content and early releases.

Pros: Pros include its superior audio quality and exclusive artist content and events.

Cons: Cons include a higher subscription cost, as well as smaller user base compared to competitors.

Use for Music Artists: Tidal is great for high-quality audio streaming. It is yet another platform that is great for discovering new and emerging artists.

Website: https://www.tidal.com

Deezer

Features: Deezer playlists include Flow: a personalised soundtrack that is based on user preferences and Daily Recommendations: new music suggestions tailored to user taste.

It also includes custom playlists that are generated from user listening habits.

Deezer's unique selling propositions include its strong focus on personalised music discovery.

Pros: Great things about Deezer include its easy-to-use interface, and also its good balance of popular and niche music recommendations.

Cons: The not-so-good points about Deezer include heavy advertising in the free version. Some features will require a premium subscription.

Use for Music Artists: Deezer is another platform that is great for discovering music tailored to user preferences. It is also great for creating personalised music experiences.

Website: https://www.deezer.com

Last.fm

Features: Last.fm is known for providing playlists based on listening habits such as its personalised radio and Recommendations. This latter algorithmic playlist is its new music suggestions based on similar artists.

Last.fm's unique selling propositions include its detailed tracking of listening habits across multiple platforms and not only on Last.fm.

Pros: Last.fm offers comprehensive music tracking and it's a good music discovery features.

Cons: The interface can be confusing for new users. It also has limited functionality without scrobbling.

Use for Music Artists: Last.fm is great for tracking and analysing listening habits, as well as discovering new music based on detailed user data.

Website: https://www.last.fm

SoundCloud

Features: SoundCloud offers its own version of Discover Weekly. Like Spotify's offering, this is a personalised playlist based on user listening habits. SoundCloud also offers its charts. These are trending music based on user engagement. Related Tracks recommends new music based on a currently playing track.

SoundCloud includes a large library of independent and emerging artists.

Pros: SoundCloud is great for introducing independent and underground music. It also has an active community of creators and listeners.

Cons: SoundCloud includes advertising in the free version. Some of the tracks may also have lower audio quality.

Use for Music Artists: SoundCloud is great for people who are looking for new and emerging artists. It is also great if you want to engage with a community of music creators and fans. Therefore, it is an appealing option for finding collaboration partners.

Website: https://www.soundcloud.com

Marketing and Promotion

HubSpot

Features: HubSpot offers an AI-powered customer relationship management (CRM) system. It enables marketing automation, email marketing and social media management. HubSpot's analytics and reporting tools are also excellent.

HubSpot's biggest strength is its comprehensive all-in-one platform for marketing, sales, and customer service and robust integration with various tools and platforms.

Pros: Plus points go to HubSpot for its user-friendly interface, extensive resources and support. It is also scalable for businesses of all sizes.

Cons: HubSpot can be expensive for smaller businesses. It also has a steeper learning curve for advanced features.

Use for Music Artists: HubSpot is ideal for creating, managing, and optimising marketing campaigns. It is useful for automating email marketing and tracking customer interactions.

Website: https://hubspot.com

Marketo (Adobe)

Features: Marketo includes AI-driven lead management and customer engagement, along with email marketing automation, analytics and account-based marketing and personalisation.

Marketo's key strengths lie in its deep integration with Adobe products, advanced segmentation and targeting capabilities.

Pros: Marketo has powerful analytics and reporting along with customizable workflows and automations.

Cons: Marketo has a high cost for small businesses, as well as complex setup and configuration.

Use for Music Artists: Marketo is effective for targeted email campaigns and lead nurturing. It is also suitable for large enterprises with complex marketing needs.

Website: https://marketo.com

Mailchimp

Features: Mailchimp incorporates AI-powered email marketing and automation, audience segmentation and predictive analytics, as well as social media posting and ad campaigns.

Mailchimp is a wise choice for its easy-to-use platform with drag-and-drop email builder, and its comprehensive free plan for small businesses.

Pros: Mailchimp includes affordable pricing tiers and extensive template library.

Cons: Cons include limited advanced features in the free plan. Also, it may not scale well for very large enterprises.

Use for Music Artists: Mailchimp is ideal for small to medium-sized businesses for email marketing and automating follow-up emails and segmenting audiences.

Website: https://mailchimp.com

Hootsuite

Features: Hootsuite has an AI-driven social media management and scheduling service along with content curation and analytics. It is also good for social listening and monitoring.

Hootsuite's unique selling propositions are its support of multiple social media platforms in one place. It also offers robust analytics and reporting tools.

Pros: Good things about Hootsuite are its user-friendly interface and its extensive integrations with other tools.

Cons: Hootsuite has higher pricing for advanced features and it also has limited features in the free plan.

Use for Music Artists: HootSuite is useful for scheduling social media posts and managing multiple accounts. It's also effective for monitoring brand mentions and social engagement.

Website: https://hootsuite.com

Sprout Social

Features: Sprout Social has AI-powered social media management and analytics, social listening and audience engagement tools, as well as content planning and publishing.

Sprout Social is best in its in-depth social listening capabilities, and its comprehensive analytics and reporting.

Pros: Plus points are due for its intuitive user interface and excellent customer support.

Cons: On the not-so-great side is the fact that Sprout Social is expensive for smaller businesses.

Some features may also be redundant for casual users.

Use for Music Artists: Sprout Social is ideal for businesses focusing on social media strategy and analytics. It is equally great for understanding audience sentiment and improving engagement.

Website: https://sproutsocial.com

SEMrush

Features: SEMRush includes AI-driven SEO along with content marketing tools, keyword research, competitive analysis, and backlink tracking. It is also known for its content optimization and marketing analytics.

SEMRush's key strengths lie in its comprehensive suite of SEO and SEM tools along with detailed competitor analysis and insights.

Pros: SEMRush has a robust feature set for SEO and digital marketing. Membership also includes regular updates and new features.

Cons: SEMRush can be overwhelming for beginners, and also expensive for small businesses.

Use for Music Artists: SEMRush is useful for optimising website content and improving search engine rankings. It is also effective for tracking and analysing competitor strategies.

Website: https://semrush.com

AdRoll

Features: Adroll includes AI-driven retargeting and display advertising, as well as cross-channel campaign management and dynamic ads and email marketing.

Adroll has a focus on retargeting and personalised ads. It also integrates with various marketing platforms.

Pros: Adroll is easy to set up and manage campaigns. It also includes comprehensive analytics and performance tracking.

Cons: Adroll has a higher cost for advanced features and it has limited customisation options for ads.

Use for Music Artists: Adroll is ideal for businesses looking to retarget website visitors and improve conversion rates. It is also useful for managing multi-channel ad campaigns.

Website: https://www.adroll.com/

Intellectual Property Management

Plagiarism Detection

Turnitin

Features: Turnitin comprises comprehensive plagiarism detection, grading and feedback tools. It also integrates with LMS (Learning Management Systems).

Turnitin is widely used in educational institutions. Therefore, it is very much trusted and also includes an extensive database of academic papers.

Pros: On the plus side, Turnitin includes accurate and reliable detection. It also provides detailed originality reports.

Cons: On the not-quite-so-hot side, it is expensive for individual users. It is also primarily geared towards educational institutions.

Use for Music Artists: Turnitin is more widely used for academic institutions and educators to check student submissions for originality. Therefore, it may not be your first choice for checking plagiarism of your music.

Website: https://www.turnitin.com

Grammarly

Features: Although it is more widely known for its ability to check grammar and spelling, Grammarly also includes plagiarism detection and also style checking. You will also find integration with browsers and word processors.

Grammarly's key unique selling point lies in its combination of grammar checking with plagiarism detection. However, it also comes complete with a very user-friendly interface.

Pros: Grammarly is easy to use. It also provides writing enhancement suggestions.

Cons: Grammarly has limited plagiarism detection compared to dedicated tools. It requires a premium subscription for full features.

Use for Music Artists: Grammarly is more suitable for writers and professionals to ensure originality and improve writing quality.

Website: https://www.grammarly.com

Copyscape

Features: Copyscape provides web-based plagiarism detection as well as batch search and API for developers.

Copyscape is specialised in online content plagiarism detection and has simple and quick checks.

Pros: It is effective for checking online plagiarism, and also has affordable pricing for individual searches.

Cons: The software is limited to web content and has no grammar checking features.

Use for Music Artists: Copyscape is ideal for content creators, bloggers, and webmasters to detect copied content online.

Website: https://www.copyscape.com

Unicheck

Features: This is a plagiarism detection with Integration for LMS and detailed similarity reports.

Unicheck has real-time search and reporting along with high integration capability.

Pros: It comes complete with accuracy and fast detection, as well as comprehensive reports.

Cons: Unfortunately, Unicheck requires subscription for full features. It is also mainly focused on academic use - hence the name.

Use for Music Artists: Unicheck is suitable for educational institutions and businesses needing reliable plagiarism detection.

Website: https://unicheck.com

Plagscan

Features: Plagscan comes complete with Plagiarism detection, document manager and reports, as well as API and LMS integration.

The software's key strengths lie in its strong privacy protections and detailed document analysis.

Pros: Plagscan has comprehensive detection with good privacy controls and flexible pricing plans.

Cons: The software may be too complex for individual users. It also focuses heavily on academic content.

Use for Music Artists: Plagscan is ideal for academic and corporate environments where document confidentiality is important.

Website: https://www.plagscan.com

Quetext

Features: Quetext includes plagiarism detection with its DeepSearch technology and citation assistant.

Quetext's unique selling proposition lies in its advanced DeepSearch for more accurate detection and user-friendly interface with citation tools.

Pros: With accurate and detailed reports, Quetext is easy to use with its helpful citation feature.

Cons: Unfortunately, Quetext is limited in its free version. The premium version also requires a subscription.

Use for Music Artists: Quetext is useful for writers, students, and professionals who require originality and proper citation in their work..

Website: https://www.quetext.com/

Small SEO Tools Plagiarism Checker

Features: With free plagiarism detection, text and file upload options and percentage-based originality score, that this software comes into its own.

The great thing about Small SEO Tools Plagiarism Checker includes the fact that it is free to use with no subscription required. It is also simple and accessible.

Pros: Small SEO Tools Plagiarism Checker is cost-effective for individual users and easy to use with quick results.

Cons: There are limited features compared to paid tools. It's less accurate for complex documents too.

Use for Music Artists: This software is most suitable for individuals and small businesses looking for a basic, free plagiarism check.

Website:
https://www.smallseotools.com/plagiarism-checker/

Rights Management

Jaxsta

Features: Jaxsta provides a comprehensive music credit database. It also provides official credit information sourced directly from labels, publishers, and industry associations. To round it off, Jaxsta also includes analytics and insights into song performance.

Perhaps, its biggest strengths lie in its verified and official music credits, and robust data integration with industry partners.

Pros: These include Jaxsta's accurate and reliable credit information as well as extensive database covering a wide range of music professionals.

Cons: Biggest cons include the facts that Jaxsta is primarily focused on credit information rather than full rights management. It is also limited to the data provided by its partners.

Use for Music Artists: Artists can verify and showcase their credits, ensuring proper attribution. The other major use for Jaxsta is the fact that it can find useful credit information for industry professionals.

Website: https://jaxsta.com

Revelator

Features: Revelator features a comprehensive rights management platform and real-time royalty tracking and analytics. It also features blockchain-based digital rights ledger and automated royalty payments.

The software provides an end-to-end rights management solution with blockchain technology and real-time data and transparent royalty tracking.

Pros: It ensures transparency and security with blockchain and also automates complex rights and royalty processes.

Cons: Revelator requires an understanding of blockchain technology. There is also a higher cost for advanced features.

Use for Music Artists: Artists can manage their rights, track royalties, and ensure fair compensation. Another major use is for independent artists and labels to streamline royalty payments.

Website: https://revelator.com

Muso.AI

Features: Muso AI features AI-driven music data analytics. It also tracks credits, streams, and social media performance. Furthermore, there is provision for detailed insights and reports.

Muso.AI combines credit tracking with performance analytics and a user-friendly interface with comprehensive insights.

Pros: There is an easy to use interface with detailed visual reports. It can also provide a holistic view of music performance and credits.

Cons: Muso.AI is primarily focused on analytics rather than direct rights management. Therefore, it is dependent on the accuracy of external data sources.

Use for Music Artists: Artists can monitor their music's performance across various platforms as well as use the app for gaining insights into audience engagement and market trends.

Website: https://muso.ai

Kobalt Music

Features: Kobalt provides music publishing and rights management with automated royalty collection and distribution. There is also detailed financial reporting and analytics.

It features an advanced technology platform for efficient rights management, and strong industry relationships with a global reach.

Pros: Kobalt runs efficient and timely royalty payments with comprehensive reporting and transparency.

Cons: Limitations include the fact that it primarily caters to established artists and larger catalogues. There is also limited accessibility for independent artists.

Use for Music Artists: Artists can manage their publishing rights and receive timely royalties. It can also be useful for large catalogues of music that need efficient rights management.

Website: https://kobaltmusic.com

Blokur

Features: Features include a blockchain-based music rights and royalties platform. There is a rights conflict resolution and claim management solution behind Blokur. It also includes data reconciliation and automated royalty distribution.

Blokur's unique selling propositions are its blockchain for secure and transparent rights management and its focus on resolving rights conflicts with accurate royalty distribution.

Pros: Pros include a secure and tamper-proof record of rights, along with efficient conflict resolution and accurate payments.

Cons: The blockchain technology may be complex for some users. It is also a relatively new platform with evolving features.

Use for Music Artists: Artists can ensure accurate rights attribution and receive fair royalties. It is great for resolving disputes and managing complex rights data.

Website: https://blokur.com

Songtrust

Features: Songtrust features global music publishing administration, royalty collection from over 60 countries, and detailed royalty reports and analytics.

However, its key strength lies in its extensive global reach for royalty collection and easy registration process for independent artists.

Pros: Songtrust simplifies global royalty collection with transparent and detailed reporting.

Cons: Service fees on Songtrust may be a consideration for smaller artists. There is also more of a focus on publishing, and not on master rights.

Use for Music Artists: Artists can register their songs and collect global royalties. Songtrust is also useful for independent artists and small publishers to maximize earnings.

Website: https://www.songtrust.com/

Performance Enhancement

Live Sound Engineering

d&b audiotechnik Soundscape

Features: Soundscape combines 3D sound design and spatial audio technology with real-time sound optimization using AI. It also integrates with d&b's hardware for seamless operation.

Soundscape's unique selling proposition is in its immersive audio experience with spatial sound and comprehensive control over sound environment.

Pros: Soundscape includes high-quality immersive sound. It integrates well with existing d&b audiotechnik systems and is great for enhancing live performances with spatial audio.

Cons: On the downside, Soundscape has higher cost due to hardware integration. It is also primarily designed for users of d&b systems.

Use for Music Artists: Soundscape is most suitable for large-scale concerts, immersive theatres, and installations requiring spatial audio.

Website: https://www.dbaudio.com

iZotope Neutron

Features: iZotope Neutron includes AI-assisted mixing and mastering tools, real-time track analysis and adjustment, as well as intelligent EQ, compression, and transient shaping.

The biggest unique selling point for iZotope Neutron is its comprehensive suite of AI-powered audio tools, as well as simplified complex mixing tasks with machine learning.

Pros: iZotope Neutron has powerful and versatile audio processing, a user-friendly interface and it reduces the need for extensive manual adjustments.

Cons: iZotope Neutron is best suited for studio use, with some live sound applications. It also requires integration with a DAW.

Use for Music Artists: It is most suitable for use by live sound engineers who also work in studio environments because it provides consistency between live and recorded sound.

Website: https://www.izotope.com

Bose Professional ControlSpace EX

Features: Bose Professional provides AI-driven audio DSP (Digital Signal Processing) with real-time audio tuning and room optimization. It is also integrated with Bose professional audio hardware.

Biggest plus points are found in Bose's seamless integration with Bose hardware for optimal performance and AI-driven adjustments tailored to the acoustics of the venue.

Pros: Further plus points for its high-quality audio performance, simplified process of tuning live sound systems and reliable and consistent results.

Cons: Bose drops points for the primary use of being of most benefit users with Bose hardware. It has a higher cost due to professional-grade equipment.

Use for Music Artists: Bose is perfect for professional live sound environments such as concert halls, theatres, and large venues using Bose systems.

Website: https://pro.bose.com

Visuals and Lighting

LightAct

Features: LightAct provides real-time 3D visualisation and projection mapping. It also integrates with Unreal Engine for immersive visuals and supports multiple inputs and outputs for complex shows.

LightAct's unique selling proposition is in its seamless integration with Unreal Engine which allows for high-quality, interactive visuals.

Pros: LightAct has a high level of customization, suitable for large-scale productions. It also supports complex interactions and triggers.

Cons: LightAct has a steeper learning curve. Therefore, it may not be suitable for the technophobic or those wishing to use a more user-friendly option. It also requires powerful hardware.

Use for Music Artists: Ideally, LightAct is best used for concerts, theatre productions, and large-scale events where high-quality, interactive visuals are needed.

Website: https://lightact-systems.com/

Notch

Features: Notch includes real-time graphics and VFX creation and integrates with various lighting consoles and video servers. Furthermore, Notch is node-based workflow for designing interactive visuals.

The best thing about Notch is its combination with real-time graphics, interactive and live performance capabilities.

Pros: Pros include high flexibility and creative control, along with real-time rendering for immediate feedback and an extensive library of effects and tools.

Cons: Notch has an expensive price point if you require the full features of the software. It also requires knowledge of node-based programming.

Use for Music Artists: The ideal use is for live concerts, interactive installations, and broadcast graphics.

Website: https://www.notch.one/

TouchDesigner

Features: TouchDesigner has real-time interactive multimedia content creation. It also supports 3D modelling, audio, and video processing, as well as extensive support for various input devices and protocols.

TouchDesigner is a highly versatile tool that integrates various types of media and interactions in real-time.

Pros: TouchDesigner is open-ended and highly customizable. It also has a large and active user community and a free version is available that has most features.

Cons: TouchDesigner can be considered as complex to learn for beginners. There are also some features that require a paid licence.

Use for Music Artists: TouchDesigner is ideal for creating interactive installations, live performance visuals, and experimental media art.

Website: https://derivative.ca/

Resolume

Features: Resolume boasts real-time VJ software for live video mixing. It integrates with MIDI controllers and DMX lighting and has a wide range of effects and transitions.

The best thing about Resolume is its Combination of powerful video mixing capabilities with extensive lighting control.

Pros: Resolume has a user-friendly interface, strong support for live performance scenarios and an extensive library of effects and plugins.

Cons: Resolume may be limited for more complex 3D visual needs. It also has a higher cost for full features.

Use for Music Artists: Resolume is perfect for DJs, VJs, and live performers who need fully robust video mixing and lighting control.

Website: https://resolume.com/

HeavyM

Features: HeavyM combines real-time projection mapping software with built-in effects and templates for quick setup. It also integrates with MIDI and OSC for interactive control.

HeavyM's biggest selling point is its user-friendly interface which is designed for quick and intuitive projection mapping.

Pros: Good things about Heavy M include the fact that it is easy to use with minimal setup time. It is also suitable for both beginners and professionals and has affordable pricing options.

Cons: Biggest limitations include the fact that it has limited advanced features compared to some competitors. It is very expensive and low-budget users would be unable to afford it.

Use for Music Artists: HeavyM is great for events, art installations, and live shows where quick and effective projection mapping is needed.

Website: https://heavym.net/

Emotional Analysis

Mood Detection

Moodagent

Features: Moodagent is an AI-driven mood-based music playlists with adjustable mood sliders for customization and personalised recommendations based on listening habits.

It offers dynamic mood sliders for precise playlist control and integration with popular music streaming services.

Pros: Moodagent offers highly customizable playlists. It also continuously learns and adapts to user preferences.

Cons: Moodagent requires integration with external streaming services. Furthermore, you will require a subscription if you require all the features.

Use for Music Artists: Moodagent is most suited for creating mood-specific playlists for various activities or events.

Website: https://moodagent.com

Moodelizer

Features: Moodelizer includes AI-generated mood-based music creation, adjustable mood parameters for real-time music adaptation and integration with video editing and media creation tools.

The biggest selling proposition is in its real-time music adaptation based on mood settings. It is also designed for use in multimedia projects.

Pros: Moodelizer incorporates high flexibility in mood-based music creation and easy integration with other media tools.

Cons: Unfortunately, Moodelizer is limited to media creation and editing contexts. It is also monetized through a subscription service which will give users the full features.

Use for Music Artists: Moodelizer is ideal for video editors and content creators needing mood-specific music.

Website: https://moodelizer.com

Chapter 10: Social Media

Facebook

It doesn't matter what your industry is, if it exists it has a presence on Facebook. With over three billion users, Facebook is still the biggest social media platform known to man. Why is this? How did Facebook grow so big?

Initially, when Mark Zuckerberg first opened Facebook, he did so in order to obtain the contact details for women he wanted to flirt with. It sounds a bit sleazy, but that's how Mr Zuckerberg first saw his creation.

Nowadays, people from all walks of life are active on Facebook. Perhaps another reason why Facebook became so big was because it does not have any of the restrictions of the other social media sites. For instance, Twitter only accepts smaller video files and a little bit of text. You can't connect with someone on LinkedIn unless you have their email address. YouTube only accepts video files. Pinterest does not allow for a lot of free flowing text. Facebook allows for all of this.

As well as having the freedom to include what you want in your Facebook posts, there is also superb targeting available. If you were a New York rock band looking for a base guitar player in New York City, you can target base players in New York City. If you wanted to target your best mate (you wouldn't, but you could) target their age, likes, occupation, interests, marital status, gender and of course their exact location. Therefore, if the base player lived in Brooklyn, New York, you can target Brooklyn.

Facebook Pages Vs Facebook Groups

You will be expected to have a Facebook page and a Facebook group for your music. Each of these has its own strengths and weaknesses. In this chapter, we will explore those strengths and weaknesses and give you some ideas that you can proceed with.

Benefits of Facebook Pages

Facebook pages are more suitable for a business if they are using it to connect with customers and build an audience. You can use your page with Facebook Advertising. It is easy to advertise for likes. You can also boost certain posts. Therefore, you can reach thousands of people and generate interest from any demographics that you choose.

Another plus point for Facebook pages is that admins do not have to link their personal profiles to the page unless they wish to. It means that you can keep your personal space and your business separate. Otherwise, you would find that people would contact you via your personal profile and you may not appreciate that.

As your following grows, you will also find that your analytics become more and more detailed. However, this is all dependent on the popularity of your content and your marketing approach.

There is also the option to schedule a post on a Facebook page for a future time and date. The good thing about this is that you can set your content to be published at the best times of the day or week. Therefore, you can expect a greater degree of success and a lot more engagement of your posts.

A Note About Facebook Advertising

Countries such as the United States, Canada, Australia and the United Kingdom are the most expensive places in which to advertise. If you don't mind where you get your likes from, I would highly advise you to choose developing countries such as India, South Africa and Brazil. In those latter countries, you can expect to pay two or three cents per like.

However, if you wish to advertise in the United States, Canada, Australia and the United Kingdom, you will be more likely to get a higher quality like. People will be more likely to spend money with you and you will have a better experience as a result.

Disadvantages of Facebook Pages

If you are not active in your page for a long period of time, Facebook will automatically consider that it is dead and set it to inactive. This may mean that you need to start all over again and build your audience from scratch.

There is no such thing as a private page. Therefore, if you require a page to have a certain level of privacy, you will be disappointed. People will be able to view the content of your page.

It is a sad fact that people may abuse your company by misusing social media channels to impersonate you. This may mean that you receive negative press as people may believe that the imposter is you. However, with a lot of public figures who experience imposters, the numbers don't tally. Someone like King Charles, Boris Johnson or David Beckham would have more than a couple of hundred likes. If you see such a page that belongs to a celebrity, you should automatically recognise that the page is fraudulent.

Advantages of Facebook Groups

There are some distinct advantages of having a Facebook group. Firstly, you have more control over the privacy of members and posts in a group. You get to decide who can post and if you don't like a post, you can remove it.

Not only do you get to control the privacy of members and posts, you also get to control what happens in the group. You make up the rules. You can impose whatever rules you want in your group. Therefore, you have total control over the content. You also get to evict any group member if they don't comply with your rules.

Disadvantages of Facebook Groups

Facebook and Instagram have the poorest reach of any of the big social media sites. This is reflected in Facebook Groups. Just as the reach is poor, the monetization of a Facebook group is limited too.

As your group gets larger, you may find that the moderation of your group gets more difficult to determine too. Therefore, you may want to look for more group admins. Your new group admins may in turn, consider your rules to be a bit harsh and start to bend the rules as they see fit. If this is the case, your group can quickly become out of control. It is like employing an untidy gardener who doesn't really care about cutting the grass.

Another negative aspect, and perhaps the most severe, is that your privacy will be compromised. If you want to keep your personal life and the life of your business separate, you will be disappointed as people will be contacting you when you just want to switch off and take a break

Facebook Advertising

As we have already mentioned Facebook Advertising for Facebook likes, we already know that Facebook likes are going to be cheaper if we target poorer countries. We also know that you can target anyone with any demographic data in any geographic location, right down to your neighbourhood. Therefore, we are going to discuss the areas of Facebook Advertising that we haven't already mentioned.

If you want to target traffic to go to your squeeze page or to purchase your product there are ways of doing this without losing more money than you are gaining. If you use pixel advertising, you can basically turn Facebook into your own super-affiliate. When your customers purchase a product from your website, Facebook earns a commission.

The negative side to pixel advertising is that it is very technical. If you are a non-techie (like me), you will find that it is a real headache trying to get your head around it all.

You should also be aware that driving traffic away from Facebook will cost you more money than advertising for Facebook likes. Facebook wants more people to use their site than they want being driven away from their site. You can expect an affiliate payment to be of dollars or pounds rather than cents or pennies.

It is also possible to pay for impressions. However, this is a risky business too. You can quickly run out of impressions, without an order and no positive difference. In this case it is worth split testing your advertising to see which works best and then run with the best option. However, when you do discover the best option, it is best to change the advertising type to pixel marketing.

If you are unsure of how to do pixel marketing, you should search for an answer on YouTube which I am going to mention next.

YouTube

YouTube is one of my favourite channels for building a social media audience. I used to feel unconfident with myself on video. However, I have been using a voiceover for a while now and it works great for what I require. You can check out my channel by searching for Krannaken TV on YouTube. It has a big "K". You can't miss it.

The reason that video is such a great way to market is that you are building a connection with your audience that you can't gain in any other form of media. You can write from your personality and include your own point of view in writing, but it is not the same as actually being there in person. You are building firm foundations when you can be there in person.

As a subscriber to various YouTube channels on a variety of subjects, I find that it is as much about the entertainment as it is about the education. Yes, you want to be educated, but most of the time you want that learning to be a fun experience. Of course, there are subjects that demand a more serious approach, but a lot of the time you want to be entertained by your viewing experience.

Another reason I watch so much on YouTube is that I find it is a key way in which to learn. It has been scientifically proven that watching a video is altogether more powerful and people learn a lot more by watching the solutions to their technical, or whatever other problems they may be facing.

One of the best things about building a YouTube audience is that you can generate income from your audience by allowing YouTube to run advertisements on your channel. This really helps to generate some real cash flow. However, at the time of writing you need a minimum of 500 subscribers and 3,000 hours of watch time in the last 12 months. You can also get into the Associates Programme and start monetizing your money by having 3 million shorts views in the past 90 days. These figures are no mean feat and although I currently have more than 500 subscribers, I don't have anywhere near enough watch time yet.

There are more ways of monetizing your YouTube channel and we will cover them in the next chapter.

Ideas For Your YouTube Channel

You may think that the content that a music YouTube channel covers could be limited. However, nothing could be further from the truth. There is a lot you can do to make your channel more popular and attract more subscribers.

With Krannaken TV (our own channel), most of what I create is my blog posts with an AI voiceover and relevant stock footage. I find that the AI voiceover has a lot clearer voice than me with no need for err's and uhmm's. It gives an all-round better impression than I do on my own.

Older videos cover anything from studio sessions with FL Studio to plugin reviews, template walkthroughs and everything in between. If you are unfamiliar with FL Studio, you should know that it is probably the most widely used digital audio workstation on the market. This is for a couple of reasons. Firstly, it is easy to use and is simple, common-sense stuff. Then there is the fact that if you purchase the Producer Edition, you get all future versions free of charge. Let me go over each of these in turn.

Music Marketing Strategies

I love the learning and the marketing sides of music. It is what I want to do and that is my plan for the future. However, as a musician, I also want to earn passive income from production music library work. I will mention that in a more detailed way in a later chapter.

I love being able to help people by suggesting solutions to their problems. I am active in various Facebook music marketing groups. It is such a pleasure if I can offer a solution to someone's concerns. For instance, one of my videos is about how to get your music on Spotify music playlists for free. I love being able to offer this advice because it helps others.

VST Plugin Reviews

One way in which you can monetize your YouTube channel is through making review videos for either software synths or effects. You could just say a few words about the software and then turn the microphone off so that your subscribers can achieve a greater listening experience and just play with the plugin for a while. I will basically completely mess around with it and see what noises, bells and whistles each plugin makes.

I can monetize this because I leave my affiliate link in the description. I also suggest that you leave a line of text at the bottom of the screen to say it is available from the affiliate link in the description.

Another good move here is to make it clear on both the video and in the video description that you are an affiliate of the product and by purchasing the product, your viewers are also supporting your channel.

Studio Sessions

This is an idea that I picked up from Mikas at WeMakeDanceMusic. In Mikas's videos, he gives a commentary while he makes a track right there on the WMDM YouTube channel. It appears that WMDM have now gone out of business, but it's a good idea to keep checking back.

The only downside to this is that it takes forever to render and upload. You spend a lot of time "goofing around" as Deadmau5 often puts it.

Why Not Offer A Freebie Friday

In the past, I have given away stuff on my YouTube channel on a Friday. I call this Freebie Friday. I've not actually done this for some time, but ideas are still bubbling away in the back of my mind.

When I used to do this regularly, I would often create sample packs of one-shot hits, loops and midi files. Sometimes, I would create a track especially and give away either a template or a sample pack with the same samples that I used in the track.

I made this free for the week until the following Friday. When that day comes around, I would put the price up, but offer another freebie in its place. Therefore, I am still monetizing my blog if my readers and viewers want to purchase something that has passed. However, there is still motivation to visit my blog because there is a freebie available.

Another thing I would give away was synth presets. This can in turn be monetized if people want to use the synth that they are for. However, I would suggest that sample packs are the best way to go. This is because sample packs can be used on any DAW without the need to purchase an entire softsynth.

Interview Videos

If you have ever been interviewed for TV or radio, you can add your interview as an mp4 video to YouTube. You may think that a radio interview can't be added as a YouTube video, but many musical personalities add their audios to YouTube with a still image of either themselves or their logo. This should be accompanied by the title of the interview.

Behind the Scenes Footage

Being a musician is often about building a relationship with your fans. You want them to consider you as a friend. Friends are interested in what each other is up to. Therefore, shooting a behind-the-scenes video is a great idea for your music. If you go away on holiday, you can shoot a video of where you're staying. This strategy really helps to build rapport with your fans.

Third Party Apps That Work Well With YouTube

In this chapter, I am going to talk about the apps that I have particular experience of. By the term app, I mean software applications. This is any piece of software or any internet service that helps the Youtuber to achieve a greater level of success.

Camtasia

Camtasia is my personal favourite program for editing and filming videos. When I switched from a Windows PC to an Apple Mac, I found it difficult to find something that would record the system sound to a high quality standard. My purchase of Camtasia was really a shot in the dark on whether or not it would record the system audio.

I know that for the Windows PC, I could use Camtasia and record the system audio. Therefore, I reasoned that it would probably do the same on an Apple Mac. I was right. I can get great quality sounding audio from recording the system itself without having the microphone pick anything up. You can actually choose whether to use the system audio, external microphone or both.

Many of my YouTube videos for Krannaken TV used to start with me talking using the external microphone. I would then switch off the microphone and turn on the system sound recorder. The result of this is that my viewers have a much better experience.

Camtasia: https://www.techsmith.com/camtasia/

Revoicer

For a long time now, I have switched to using Revoicer and Canva (which we'll talk about later). Revoicer provides me with the most realistic AI voiceovers you can imagine. Therefore, I can make my videos clear to understand and more professional as a result.

Revoicer is available at https://revoicer.com/

WeVideo

WeVideo is an online video recorder that can be used instead of Camtasia to record your screen and anything you choose to record with it. However, I found that it did not record the system audio to a suitable enough standard. If I just got it wrong, it was because I have minimal experience with it. In that case, it could be easier to use it. Camtasia is a doddle compared to anything else I have seen including WeVideo.

Maybe the best aspect of WeVideo, for me, is that it is online. This means you can access your account from any computer with an internet connection and you still have your content stored so that you can continue to work on it. That is the unique selling point for WeVideo.

WeVideo is available at https://www.wevideo.com/

VidIQ

Uploading videos to YouTube is done through a dialogue box and it is a much more involved process. This ensures that certain aspects of your videos gain more focus.

I now use the premium version of VidIQ and I trust it because my viewer numbers are sky-rocketing lately. Quite a few of the videos get hundreds of streams while almost all have above 50 streams after a few days.

The AI generator on VidIQ has been a Godsend. It gives me the title, the text and the keywords as well as some options for the thumbnail. I couldn't be happier with it. I have achieved so much more and built some significant numbers due to using VidIQ.

I can highly recommend it to anyone with a YouTube channel.

At times, the keyword research has looked off. I can admit that, but I trusted VidIQ and it is delivering much better than I ever could have expected.

Find VidIQ at https://vidiq.com/

Canva

I use Canva for absolutely everything now. I created the cover of this book with Canva. I also create everything for my video as well as my blog banners with Canva.

Perhaps the best thing about Canva, other than the range of visuals that I can create with it, are the choice of designs available and the ability to customise them so that they are of a much higher standard. You are going to need the best thumbnail that you can get if you hope to maximise the number of views you get on YouTube and you can get that with ease here.

Canva is not free. It's something like $79 per year, but I can afford that easily and I would be happy to pay twice that to get the use out of Canva that I do.

Find Canva at https://www.canva.com/

Growing Your YouTube Following

There are a few ways in which you can grow your list of subscribers on YouTube. In this chapter, I am going to let you know about the good ways to build your subscriber-base as a musician. I am also going to point out the ways that are not so good and tell you why they are not so good.

With Krannaken TV, we build our channel with the help of VidIQ and Hypeddit.

Hypeddit is a way to grow your email list and your following on other social media sites too. I have used Hypeddit to grow my email list, YouTube subscribers and my SoundCloud followers. The good thing about growing my YouTube numbers through Hypeddit is that the people who subscribe to my channel this way, are all interested in making music. This book is for musicians and I aim my website at musicians. Therefore, Hypeddit can offer me the perfect market.

The way to grow your subscriber list that is not as good is the way I have just mentioned, is through sub-for-sub. The thing with sub-for-sub is that your subscribers are not targeted. They could be interested in anything and are not necessarily interested in the subject matter that you make videos about. However, this is the easiest way to gain subscribers and if you are just looking for numbers and not quality, sub-for-sub could help. I don't recommend sub-to-sub at all though. It is better to have 10 interested subscribers than 100 subscribers who may not even understand your language. Sub-for-subs quickly drop off.

Consistency is Key

One of the most important qualities to have with either a YouTube channel or a blog, is consistency. You need to keep making great videos for your channel. I publish new content on my blog and on my YouTube channel, three times per week. I also turn the videos into YouTube shorts so that I can generate even more views.

Another good idea is to set a different kind of day for a different kind of video. For instance, on one day, you can do a VST plugin review. This can be you introducing the plugin with your external microphone. You would then turn off the microphone and completely mess around with the plugin. This shows your viewers exactly what they can expect from the sound quality. Furthermore, you can do this from the level you are at right now. You don't need to pretend to be a genius in music production. You can be happy to mess around and make something and also to play with the factory presets.

I suggest you check out Adam Ivy for his YouTube channel. Adam tends to rant, but his rants are especially good and he makes a clear case for everything he is talking about.

On another day, I tend to review a musical effects plugin. This is as opposed to what we've already spoken about a few moments ago. This is because you can talk about plugins such as reverb, delay, EQ, compression, etc. There are a lot more effects plugins than instrument plugins on the market. Therefore, there is always plenty to choose from.

That is how you can plan your week. Why not make the occasional on a weekend if something important comes to mind that doesn't fit into any of the days. For instance, you can make a video on a Saturday on how to install factory presets for a particular synth.

By being consistent in this way and letting your audience know of the schedule of your website, you are meeting their satisfaction and your subscriber numbers will be boosted as a result.

Social Bee

This is a service I have been using for some time. I have been using it to schedule TikTok, YouTube, LinkedIn, Facebook, Instagram and Twitter. The best thing about Social Bee is that you can schedule different kinds of posts. You can schedule your RSS feed to deliver your latest blog post. You can also schedule promotions, fun facts, competitions, etc, with absolute certainty that they will be published and when.

Find SocialBee at https://socialbee.io/

HootSuite

HootSuite is a great option for scheduling on various different social media platforms. HootSuite, like Social Bee and Buffer (which we will discuss next) is a generic social media scheduling service that is good for all the major social media platforms.

If you have a team of multiple members, HootSuite could be right for you if you require multiple people to schedule social media posts.

Buffer

If you are looking for a less expensive, no frills, basic and easy to use social media scheduling service, Buffer could well be a good option for you. Buffer allows social media scheduling on all the major platforms and it is completely reliable.

Plans start with a free option where you can manage something like 3 Facebook and Twitter posts every 24 hour period. The premium options start from $6 per month and allows for posting to Facebook, Twitter and LinkedIn.

Microcontent

In 2022, microcontent became massive news for all music artists. It became a big issue in the music industry and lots of artists were using it to grow their following organically and the three sites that changed the game to microcontent marketing were TikTok, Instagram and YouTube Shorts. However, the first platform who introduced microcontent video was Snapchat, in 2011.

What is Microcontent?

Simply put, microcontent is a clip of your video that lasts for less than one minute. As musicians, we need to make sure that that clip is the main hook of our song. That is how we are going to drive interest from people on all these different channels.

Another thing about microcontent videos is that they are always portrait (or vertical) as opposed to landscape (or horizontal). This is because they are better for mobile devices.

Let's look at each of the three platforms in turn starting with TikTok...

TikTok

The awesome thing about TikTok is the organic reach. You could put up your first video today and within a week, you can very easily see more than 200 viewers who have all watched your video.

The trick now is to be consistent and keep making new videos. You can keep the same audio, but just use a completely different stock image or video on it. This way, your music will keep fresh and you will always be able to entertain because the visuals are different each time. This gives more exposure to your music and you are able to generate more fans as a result. The more times someone sees your videos the more likely they are to like your music.

To find new visuals, I can recommend Yay Images who have a growing library of new visual assets. An account with Yay Images will set you back something like $11.99 per month or $24.99 for three months. However, if you purchase a Canva subscription, they will include videos and images in your premium account.

Instagram

I personally use Instagram less than TikTok and YouTube Shorts. However, I usually put something about my newest blog posts on Instagram. On mobile, the Instagram microcontent feature is similar to the other two platforms.

Instagram are owned by Facebook and so advertising is cheap and targeting is very sharp. This means that you can target the people who are most likely to be fans of your genre of music. If your music is similar to Armin Van Buuren or Tiesto, you can choose to target their fans by adding relevant hashtags in your posts.

YouTube Shorts

The thing I like best about YouTube Shorts is the wide variety of different microcontent you can find on the platform. It is easy to find content in a lot of different niches and genres. I also like the different film clips that you can get on YouTube Shorts.

Making the Microcontent Videos

As I have already mentioned, it is a great idea to use multiple different visuals on multiple different videos. You can find visuals at Yay Images or Canva and that is where I recommend that you look for your content. It is inexpensive, yet both sites also have a great range of different options for you to choose from.

When you make your videos, I recommend you use Camtasia. It has a user-friendly and simple interface that most people should be able to use without any issues. You can use the same videos for TikTok that you use for YouTube Shorts. However, Instagram uses different dimensions so you will have to change the size of your video to fit. The sizes for the different videos are as follows...

TikTok and YouTube Shorts - 1080 wide x 1920 tall
Instagram in-stream videos 1080 wide x 1350 tall.

Chapter 11: Being an Independent Artist Versus Being Signed to a Label

In today's music business, there is as much chance as you finding success as an independent artist as there is being signed to a record label. The latter is no longer the holy grail of the music industry. As Krannaken, we have been signed to two record labels in the past and we are currently seeing more exposure as independent artists than we would be working for a label.

The old model of the record label was that they would pay you a deposit to produce an album, EP or single. You would then arrange and record everything, paying the studio and the engineers.

The new model of the record label is that they charge the artist for representation, guidance and added exposure. They even charge the artist for music video production. Therefore, you are better to be in control of your own destiny.

Good Things to Remember About Being an Independent Artist

As already mentioned, you are better in today's world, to be an independent artist. There is a lot of corruption in the industry with artists being the ones to pay for everything.

As artists, our business acumen is just as important as our musical skills. We need to monetize, monetize, monetize as much as we can. I give you the ideas and strategies you should have in place, throughout this book. However, you can never learn too much and I urge you to continue your search for new marketing strategies, not only from forthcoming editions of this book, but from YouTube, Udemy courses, Sonic Academy, Skillshare, various magazines, etc..

When we read more information, we learn more. If we learn more, we can give better advice. When we give better advice, we become more valued as people. When we are more valued as people, we can expect a better job. Finally, when we have a better job, we can expect more money.

What does the last paragraph mean for today's musical artists? It means that when we understand more about our art, we can do more and when we practise we can build more skills. Therefore, our music will be improved as a result. When our music is improved, we will have more attention. We will have more attention so we will get more streams and sales and when we have more streams and sales, we will have more financial income.

It is exactly the same for you. My aim in writing this book is to enable you to become better at marketing your music. Do you think your music deserves to be heard? Well, I do. I believe everyone who is passionate about music has a place to make their own in the music industry. Think about the legacy you are leaving your children and their children for generations. I am excited about the thought of my great-great-grandchildren listening to my music and thinking about that relative of theirs who made it. It really is quite a thought. That is one of the best things about the music industry.

While we are talking about the financial side of things, it is important to mention that if you are not signed to a label, you get more money. The label exists just as much to make money for themselves, as they exist to support you. Money is why anyone works and a record label is no different.

Another great aspect of today's music industry is that it is open to everyone who wants to make music. Anyone can get their music heard on all the biggest music streaming and retail websites in cyberspace. How many streams or album sales you gain is purely reflected on your Spotify streams.

There are deadlines, rules and restrictions posed by a record label. That is one of the first things that you will have to agree to if you are signed to a label. They will expect you to produce x number of albums, EPs or singles. This is because they make money on each release.

As an independent artist, you make the rules. When you have enough music to go on with, you plan your releases. For Krannaken, it works particularly well as we produce a lot of music that we either want to release ourselves or submit to production music libraries. We will discuss more about production music libraries later in this book. When we feel ready to submit an EP, album or track, we just have to submit it to Distrokid and they will have it out and published (very often within 24 hours).

You will also retain copyright as an independent artist. This is a big plus point because artists very often have to relinquish their rights to a bigger stake of royalties due to the rules and restrictions placed by the label.

The Old Artist-Label Model Versus The New

In our time as Krannaken, we have been under two labels. Both of these labels required what I call "the new artist model" and that is a big part of why we choose now, to be independent.

The old model is that the label would pay the artist an advance in order to have music published. This would often go towards the hire of musical facilities and wages for session musicians, audio engineers, mastering engineers, etc. The artist or artists would end up with a much smaller cut than the money that the label initially paid.

However, the artist could expect to receive more money once the advance has been recouped by the label. Very often, the artist had too much money than they knew what to do with and that is where the drug and alcohol addiction came into the picture for many artists. Just like in any industry where young people were paid too much, the music industry is no different.

The new model is that the label will charge you somewhere in the region of £50/$65 to publish your music and they will give you some exposure as a result of being on their books. Any money that comes in from music sales or streaming would go to the artist. This model is ok if you're not expecting your music to be a full-time income. However, if you are relying on this money for your living costs, you will be disappointed. It is not enough to live on.

In order to generate the minimum wage level, you need to generate somewhere in the region of 200,000 Spotify streams per month. As many as 80% of all artists don't generate more than 50 streams per month. As Krannaken, we don't get that much. That is why I am looking at some of the income generating strategies of chapter 11 of this book.

So What is Good About Using a Label Today?

One of the best things about using a record label today is that you never know what connections that label has. You never know who you will meet, and what they will bring to the table. You could meet someone who will propel you into international stardom – if that is what you want.

As Krannaken, we just want to make an income from our music. We don't want fame or necessarily fortune. We just want to be able to live, pay our bills and support our families.

As a result of working with a label, we have gained more exposure. Club DJs have played our music to a great reception. It feels great when a floor full of clubbers is dancing to something that you created. It really is very rewarding from that point of view.

Working with a label multiplies your reach exponentially if it has the right connections. Although we have contacts ourselves, it always helps to have as many connections as possible. Like I said before, you never know who your labels will have connections with. They could be connected and able to influence large media corporations like radio and TV stations, key people at nightclub chains, etc.

Chapter 12: Distribution Channels

Both free distribution and paid distribution has pros and cons.

A free distributor has a vested interest because they only get paid when you are getting more streams. The great thing about using a free option is that nobody is going to take your music down from the sites if you are unable to keep up with a payment for any specific reason.

However, you have to bear in mind that a free service isn't making as much out of you as the paid services so they may not treat your custom as urgently and carefully as a paid alternative.

Having said that a free option has a vested interest, a paid service doesn't want to lose your custom so they will want to do the best they can for you and your music too.

Personally, I use RouteNote. I feel comfortable with them and the fact that they don't take my music down is a good reason to keep using them.

I have used Distrokid, but have had to take our music down because Distrokid were charging me a lot of extras and they wouldn't keep my music up there indefinitely unless I paid more.

List of Free Music Distribution Services

Amuse

Commission: 15% commission on the free plan
Platforms: 27 retail and streaming services
Publish Time: 28 days
Website: https://www.amuse.io

RouteNote

Commission: 15% on the free plan
Platforms: 37 streaming and download services
Publish Time: 1-3 days
Website: https://www.routenote.com

Soundrop

Commission: 15%
Platforms: 29 platforms
Publish Time: 9-15 days
Website: https://www.soundrop.com

United Masters

Commission: 10% on the free plan
Platforms: 50+ platforms
Publish Time: Varies; typically within a few days
Website: https://www.unitedmasters.com

Symphonic

Commission: 15%
Platforms: 200+ platforms
Publish Time: 4 weeks
Website: https://www.symphonicdistribution.com

TuneCore

Commission: 20% on the free plan
Platforms: Social media sites (TikTok, Facebook, Instagram, YouTube)
Publish Time: 3-9 business days
Website: https://www.tunecore.com

ONErpm

Commission: 15%
Platforms: 30+ platforms with a focus on Latin American markets
Publish Time: Varies
Website: https://www.onerpm.com

AWAL

Commission: 15%
Platforms: 30+ platforms
Publish Time: 4 weeks
Website: https://www.awal.com

List of Paid Music Distribution Services

Distrokid

Upfront Cost: $19.99/year
Commission: 0%
Platforms: 150+
Publish Time: 1-2 days
Website: https://www.distrokid.com
Details: DistroKid offers unlimited song uploads for an annual fee and is known for its fast distribution and keeping 100% of royalties.

TuneCore

Upfront Cost: $14.99 per year for the Rising Artist Plan and, $29.99 per year for the Breakout Artist Plan). There is also a Professional Plan which costs $49.99 per year.
Commission: 0% (for paid plans)
Platforms: 150+
Publish Time: 2-5 days
Website: https://www.tunecore.com
Details: TuneCore charges an annual fee with various plans and retains all royalties. The service includes robust analytics and there are also publishing administration options.

CD Baby

Upfront Cost: $9.99 per standard Single, $29.99 per standard album, and $49.99 per Pro Album
Commission: 9%
Platforms: 150+
Publish Time: 1-2 weeks
Website: https://www.cdbaby.com
Details: CD Baby charges a one-time fee per release and includes YouTube monetization and sync licensing options.

LANDR

Upfront Cost: $9 per single, $19 per album or EP, $25 per year for the Standard Plan) and $89 per year for the Pro Plan
Commission: 15% (for one-time fees)
Platforms: 250+
Publish Time: 2-4 days
Website: https://www.landr.com
Details: LANDR offers both per-release fees and annual plans. It includes mastering, collaboration tools, and extensive distribution.

Chapter 13: Websites for Musicians

Last.Fm

Last.fm have some great features that allow you to be found more easily. Firstly, there is the "scrobbling" feature that checks what users are listening to most. The artificial intelligence of Last.fm then streams the songs based on the findings. Therefore, the most popular songs get more and more streams. This is great if your song is particularly popular.

This is how Last.fm keeps people coming back. The most popular music gets the most exposure. It's a win-win for the artists gaining the exposure and the people at Last.fm.

There is also the ability for fans to subscribe to your music and once they are subscribed, they will receive an instant notification when you have published a new song. However, you can also share news updates about your music or your band.

Another way for users to find new artists to follow is by following other music fans who are interested in similar genres. They will then be notified when the people they follow have a new favourite song.

Go to https://www.last.fm/

SoundCloud

SoundCloud used to be one of my favourite music platforms. The reason for this was that I could check out the music in my genre that was published as recently as the past hour. That was one of my major reasons for using SoundCloud. However, they appear to have cancelled this feature. I believe that is a particularly bad marketing decision by SoundCloud as there were probably many other people who enjoyed the ability to find new music.

SoundCloud still have the Spotlight feature on their users profile pages. However, to use this, one needs to have a premium account. The buy link is a useful feature too.. This helps artists to gain exposure for my music.

Like, follow and repost tracks that either fit with your genre or songs that you like. Please note only like, follow and repost tracks that you really like. There is no point in sharing work that you don't like – unless you are doing that for Hypeddit which we will get to later in this chapter.
SoundCloud goes hand-in-hand with Hypeddit, but we will mention that later in this chapter.

You can access SoundCloud at https://soundcloud.com/

MixCloud

MixCloud is especially good if you are a DJ or a podcaster. It allows you to upload and share your music or podcast to the world. There are various ways you can do this and these include...

- Using hashtags to point your fans to your genre. People who are looking for your genre will then be able to find you much more easily.
- If people like your music they will follow you. This gives you much more chance of being listened to by that fan again. By following you, your listeners are choosing to listen to your show again.
- It helps to upload content to MixCloud regularly. If you have a weekly show, don't forget to upload your show every single week. If you have a daily show, you need to upload to MixCloud every day.
- Just as with any content, you need to share your MixCloud show on every social media site you are present on. I share my posts on Twitter, Facebook, Pinterest and Krannaken has a YouTube channel too.
- MixCloud have developed a WordPress plugin that you can install on your site. This allows your Mixcloud content to be streamed through your WordPress website.
- As with any social media platform, you need to get involved in what is going on. Listen to other shows. Show support for other shows by sharing them on your social media channels. If you love what you hear from a show, why not

subscribe. You can do this through MixCloud Select.

- MixCloud Select allows you to earn money from your biggest fans by allowing them to subscribe to your show. How cool is that? In subscribing, your biggest fans are paying you a monthly subscription. Payment for Select is taken from the money you generate through subscription payments. Artists and songwriters take a 65 % cut of the subscription payments. There is a 5% cut on transaction fees. That leaves 30% left. 60% of that cut goes to the DJ or podcaster and 40% goes to MixCloud.

You can find MixCloud at https://mixcloud.com/.

Patreon

Much like MixCloud, Patreon offers a subscription service so that you can be paid by your biggest fans. For a regular donation (or subscription), you have to provide your fans with additional merchandise or some freebie of some sort. This can be CDs that are only sent to Patreon subscribers. It could be a coupon code for a discount on merchandise. Patreon is easy to set up and any artist, podcaster, comedian or other performing artists can open a Patreon account. Even if you are just a YouTube personality, you can still have an account on Patreon.

Just as with MixCloud, Patreon takes a cut from subscription payments for their costs. The lowest payment is 5% and the most expensive is 12% of the money you have coming in from fans. This means there are no upfront costs.

You can access Patreon by going to https://www.patreon.com/

Hypeddit

Hypeddit is one of my favourite music marketing sites. I just love this and I get a lot more back from my subscription with them than I would get in any other way of marketing my music.

With Hypeddit, you can build your social media and music following. This is done through the building of landing pages. The person seeing the form can follow you on any of these social media and music sites…

- Facebook
- Instagram
- Twitter
- YouTube
- Deezer
- Spotify
- Twitch
- Bandcamp
- MixCloud

- SoundCloud
- Apple iTunes
- Facebook Messenger

You can also obtain names, email addresses and request a donation from the fan who is viewing your landing page.

The other amazing features on Hypeddit include the Promotion Exchange. This runs a little like the old fashioned traffic exchanges. However, they are far, far more popular and powerful than the traffic exchange ever was. On Hypeddit, the Promotion Exchange allows you to obtain details from other artists.

In exchange for giving your details and following them on various different websites, you get one credit and also a free download of the song you have just heard a clip from.

It is advised that people using the landing pages only ask for a SoundCloud share, like and follow. However, you can do much more than that. I have built my music YouTube channel and gained targeted subscribers from the music production community on Hypeddit. As my book, my blog and my YouTube channel are based on people who make music, this is my ideal source of quality subscribers.

When you use Hypeddit along with SoundCloud, you can have a link that quite clearly says "Free Download" on your SoundCloud track. Therefore, marketing through SoundCloud with your Hypeddit link allows you to gain more than just a SoundCloud like, share and follow. You can build any of your social media accounts that I mentioned in the list.

You can create unlimited landing pages and access all other features for only $9 per month. Hypeddit is available at https://hypeddit.com.

SoundPlate

SoundPlate enables you to submit music to Deezer and Spotify playlist curators. This is completely free for the artist. However, there is a charge for the playlist curator so that they can gain submissions from artists all over the world.

Genres included in SoundPlate include…

- House and electronic
- Pop and commercial
- Hip-hop and urban
- Chill-hop and beats
- Chill and ambient
- Rock and indie
- Afrobeats and afropop

- Trip-hop and electronica
- Reggae and dancehall
- Drum and bass
- Latin
- Classical and piano
- Country
- R&B and soul
- Jazz
- Other

Although SoundPlate is completely free for the artist, there is no guarantee that your submission will be accepted. It is purely down to the discretion of the playlist curator as to whether or not they accept your work.

As a playlist curator myself, I have found that a lot of the music submitted to me has been completely unsuitable for my playlists. For instance, I would be presented with a hip-hop track – even though my playlists are entirely about trance music. I am not saying the music was bad. A lot of it was of a high standard, but it just wasn't right for my playlists.

When you select your genre from the list at the top of the page, you will be presented with a grid with all the latest playlists listed in squares on the grid. Each playlist has its own square. You then click on one of the playlists and read through the submission guidelines. Here is where you will learn more about what music the curator is looking for. If you are still sure that the music is suitable for the playlist, you click on the relevant links and follow the prompts.

SoundPlate is at https://soundplate.com/

StageIt

Are you all dressed up with nowhere to go and no gig to perform? Don't worry, just go to StageIt and plan your own gigs. Fans can pay you good money to see you perform live online.

The slogan of StageIt is "The front row seat with the backstage experience". This is because fans have a better view of you than they would if they were there in an audience-packed auditorium. Not only that, your fans can actually converse with you at the same time and you can get tips for music well played.

Think about this for a second. You don't have to travel and carry heavy and expensive equipment to places where it may be stolen or damaged. You can leave it exactly where it is and film it with your desktop or laptop computer, or your mobile phone or tablet. It's as easy as that and people will come and watch you time and again.

There is no waiting for months to see your favourite artist in concert. They can perform seven nights a week online so you can stream it to your home computer.

StageIt is free for the artist to organise and hold a gig. They just take a cut of the money that you generate through ticket sales and tips. StageIt has its own currency. These are called notes and one note is ten cents. However, you can only buy them in bulk starting from 50 up to a total of 5000 notes. Therefore, this is $5 to $500 worth of notes.

Find out more about StageIt at https://www.stageit.com/

Spotify for Artists

Spotify for Artists is the place to control your Spotify profile. You can edit your About page, change the profile header and see the latest statistics.

The statistics will show information such as how many streams an artist is getting, locations of your listeners, how people are interacting with your music (whether they are adding it to their playlists, etc), the genders of our fans,

Spotify for Artists is at https://artists.spotify.com.

Sonic Academy

Since joining Sonic Academy, my music has taken a dramatic leap in the quality of the sound and what I am able to accomplish. It has tons of music production tutorials as well as their own VST plugins (ANA and Kick 2). They also have sample packs and more.

Sonic Academy is led by Steve Agnelli of Agnelli and Nelson (a late 1990s classic trance duo). That is just another reason for my interest. That was the time that I was into trance most and being trained by an organisation led by someone I idolised that much is great.

Of course, Sonic Academy isn't just about Steve Agnelli. There are tons of great producers who run courses on all aspects of trance, techno and house music production. This is right across the board and is partly how I got the idea for trancewave.

Membership to Sonic Academy starts at $10.62 per month if you purchase the annual subscription. If you pay per month, you can pay either $17.83 if you take out a monthly membership without committing to a year of Sonic Academy membership or $12.73 if you are happy to keep to a year's commitment of Sonic Academy.

Considering how much I have learned and how much my music production skills have progressed, that is a small price to pay.

You can access Sonic Academy at https://www.sonicacademy.com/

JamPlay

If you play guitar and want to improve your guitar skills in any genre you are interested in, then JamPlay is an excellent place for you to learn more. There are many great tutors and live training sessions so that a tutor can actually help you in person rather than over a video that was made months (or even years) ago.

JamPlay costs $19.95 per month. Considering everything that is included in the teaching materials, it is well worth it. If you do want to learn to play guitar, the alternative could be private tuition, which is likely to cost you more than $19.95 for a one-hour session. JamPlay is available for you whenever you want to learn.

Find JamPlay at https://jamplay.com/

Bedroom Producers Blog

Apart from Krannaken.com (of course), Bedroom Producers Blog is my favourite site to go to for fun and interesting blog posts.

If you compose and produce electronic music, I would advise you to check Bedroom Producers

Blog from time-to-time for music production news, tips and ideas.

You can find Bedroom Producers Blog here - https://bedroomproducersblog.com/

Music Think Tank

The great thing about Music Think Tank is that it is largely guided by the audience. Apart from the fact that it is more geared towards actual music marketing than the other blogs mentioned here (Bedroom Producers Blog and Sound On Sound). If you are looking for great music marketing advice, you could do worse than keeping an eye on Music Think Tank.

You can access Music Think Tank here - http://www.musicthinktank.com/

Sound-On-Sound

Another blog that is worth your attention is Sound On Sound. Initially a widely renowned magazine for the music industry, Sound On Sound provides regular updates and new posts of interest to the musical community.

Access Sound-On-Sound here - https://www.soundonsound.com/

Chapter 14: Other Ways for Music Artists to Make Money

I have already mentioned some ways to monetize your music earlier in this book. However, I would like to make some additions to it - so you will find those additions in this chapter.

Film Scoring

What is film scoring?

Have you ever wondered who wrote the music to your favourite film? Do you ever think about who writes the music for TV? The field of TV and film scoring can be difficult to break into. This is especially true for the first-timer. However, if you write great music that fits in with the subject and the atmosphere of the production, you can find yourself writing for TV and film.

There are a few things that you have to bear in mind about film scoring. You need to think about the market you are writing for, rather than what you like to write. If you are a classical composer and you want to write a piece of music for a clubbing scene, you will be disappointed to learn that your music was rejected. You need to write what you are good at. However, keep it on-spec and make sure it is right for the production.

How to get into film scoring

There are a number of ways that you can break into the world of film music. Perhaps the best way is to go to networking events. When you go to these events, it would be wise to take a copy of your past music on CD that you can leave with prospective clients.

Other ways that you can find clients for your film scoring services could be through freelancing websites. Such sites include Upwork (https://www.upwork.com/) and Freelancer (https://www.freelancer.com/).

How much does it cost to get into film scoring?

If you want to use Freelancer to find a film scoring opportunity, you will be restricted by the number of bids that you have purchased in a month. You will also have to pay 10% or £3.50 (whichever is greater). The bid packages start from £0.99 ($1.35). This plan gets you 15 bids. The most expensive is £50 and for that you get 700 bids per month.

With Upwork, you can make 60 applications per month. You will be charged 20% from $0 to $500, 10% from $500 to $10,000 and 5% for more than $10,000.

There are various different networking groups that meet offline in different geographic locations. Therefore, I am unable to advise you as I can't speak about a specific location. However, if you are looking for a good offline networking group for musicians, you may find them through Eventbrite (https://www.eventbrite.co.uk/) or Meetup (https://www.meetup.com/) Both of these sites list various offline networking groups that you can try.

The good points about film scoring…

- This is one of the most fun areas of music that you can get into.
- It is also very rewarding.
- It pays well.

The bad points about film scoring…

- There is a lot of competition
- You will undoubtedly face a lot of rejection.

Loops, Samples, Templates and Presets

How can you get into writing loops, samples, templates and presets?

There is no point me telling you what loops and samples are. That would be preaching to the converted, but all music producers and people who use digital audio workstations to make music, use samples. We all use percussive samples, effects samples and many of us use vocal samples. There is, however, a lot more to it. You can write midi files for arpeggios that will enable music creators to sound great.

This is one of the easiest areas of music to start working in. All you need is, probably, what you already have. You need a digital audio workstation. You need to have something you can record with and you need to be accomplished at processing your sounds with different effects plugins.

Making your own synth presets is just as easy, if not easier, as making loops and samples. You can choose any software synthesizer. This could be something like SoundSpot's Union, Xfer Serum or most other synths.

Templates require you to create a track inside your digital audio workstation. Therefore, this requires more work. Templates can be DAW-specific. However, if you wanted to make a template of a trance track, you would choose a DAW that you can use on both a Mac and a PC. My personal choice would be FL Studio, but that's just my preference. FL studio templates (flp) can be made on an Apple Mac and used on a Windows PC. It is exactly the same kind of file and they are not used on one and not on another. In the same way, I can use FL

Studio files on my Apple Mac that were made on a PC.

My biggest advice to you if you want to make samples, loops, presets and templates is to get yourself a WordPress.org website. This should be a theme like the one I am using at Krannaken.com. You can add your videos, audios, textual blog posts – anything and it will look great.

In the past, I have published free samples, loops, presets and I could offer templates (although I haven't given a template away yet, I could quite easily do so). If you have a "Freebie Friday" where you make something free through your website every Friday for one week.

How much does it cost to get into this business?

If you want a free theme, but a WordPress.org site, I suggest that you use NameCheap to set up a website (with a domain name and hosting). Also, if you have the money, go for the Second Line Themes at https://secondlinethemes.com/. It is also a good idea to set yourself up with a free MailChimp account for your email marketing.

Altogether, you are looking at around an initial cost of around $90 or £70 for your website. The theme costs $69. The hosting is an investment of around $5 per month and the domain is an annual payment of around $15

You may also want to spend some money on VST's, etc. The answer to this all depends on what you buy and how often you purchase new VST's. It is like asking, "How long is a piece of string?" It could be any price. This all depends on what your budget is like and how often you want to spend money on new plugins. One good thing about purchasing your VST's from Plugin Boutique is that they always have something that is free. All you need to do is purchase something else from their site and specify that you want to take advantage of the freebie.

Good points about this model…

What are the good points?

- Easy to get into
- Fairly inexpensive
- It is a lot of fun

Bad points about this model…

And the bad points include?

- You can't compromise on the quality of your work. Failure to make decent sounding products will leave people thinking you are a second rate provider.
- It can be lonely

- You may be tempted either to sell your products either too cheaply or too expensively.

Chapter 15: Further Learning

This chapter is all about learning and making sure that you keep up-to-date with all the new music marketing strategies coming in. Of course, you can keep an eye on Krannaken.com, but there is much more to it than that. You need to train yourself as a businessman, but you also need to train your musical ear if you hope to keep releasing great music. In this chapter, we will look at all the paid and free resources for you to grow in your music career.

YouTube Channels

Armada TV

Armade is the biggest trance music record label in the world with 40,000 titles. The label was first established in 2003 and since then it has won various awards. Founding DJ, Armin Van Buuren, has won numerous awards as DJ of the Year, etc.

Subscribe at: https://www.youtube.com/@armadamusictv

Music Marketing YouTube Channels

Damian Keyes
Damian has been there, done it and helped thousands of other musicians to find success with their music careers.

On the plus side, Damian's music channel is completely free, videos are in-depth and easy to follow.

And the cons: Damian talks more about guitar music and music with vocals. If that's your thing, great. However, Krannaken are an instrumental electronic outfit. Therefore, we don't sing. We don't even call our music songs. We refer to them as tracks. A song is sung so it needs vocals, but a track can be 100% instrumental like you will find in the vast majority of our music.

https://www.youtube.com/@DamianKeyes

SMART MUSIC BUSINESS

You will find Smart Music Business written in all caps like SMART MUSIC BUSINESS on YouTube. I am not prepared to shout so I'll just refer to it as Smart Music Business. The channel is owned by a really nice guy called Chris.

You may not have heard from him in the past, but Chris is also known as Manafest and has just short of 1,000,000 monthly Spotify streams. That's a fantastic amount.

Chris often talks about pumping money that you don't necessarily have into the music. However, if you do have some financial backing, you can do worse than getting advice from Chris's videos.

https://www.youtube.com/@SMARTMUSICBUSINESSVIDEOS

Stock Music Licensing

Daniel Carrizalez owns two YouTube channels. These are Daniel Carrizalez and Stock Music Licensing. Daniel's Stock Music Academy is the one we will talk about here though.

If you want to make good money in a more realistic way from your music, then stock music licensing is a fantastic option. If you have been making music for a while and don't know what to do with it, stock music licensing is a way that you can turn that music into passive income.

All of the people mentioned in this chapter are experts in their own field. Daniel is no different, but with expertise comes more expense. If you want to spend $150 on a Teachable course in stock music licensing, this is a good choice. Daniel's YouTube channel offers you free access to some great teaching though.

At the time of writing, there hasn't been a fresh video on Daniel's Stock Music Channel for three months. I hope and pray that Daniel is doing ok and that he will return to make more videos very soon. Daniel, if you are reading this, we miss you brother.

https://www.youtube.com/@StockMusicLicensing

Adam Ivy

Adam is a really entertaining guy. He will sit there (or stand there - don't know which) and rant for a few minutes. Adam's rants are famous and that is what he is known for.

On the negative side, Adam often talks so fast that you don't know what he's talking about. While his talks are always fun, you do wish that you knew what they were about.

https://www.youtube.com/@adamivy

Andrew Southworth

Andrew is a bona fide music artist who tells it from his perspective as a music artist. He uses real world examples, practices what he preaches and demonstrates this throughout his videos.

https://www.youtube.com/@AndrewSouthworth

Music Business Advice @MusicEbooks

Music Business Advice at @MusicEbooks run a YouTube channel on music marketing that run tutorials on marketing and promotion. They have also been known to promote the work of individual artists to an audience of just over 29,000 subscribers at the time of writing.

https://www.youtube.com/@MusicEbooks

Burstimo

Burstimo have been around for a while and have built up a significant image for expertise in the music scene. They know everything there is to know and their content is amazing with regular, clear and easy to follow tutorials.

https://www.youtube.com/@Burstimo

All About Helping Musicians Podcast

As you may gather from the name, this is a podcast that helps musicians with all aspects of music marketing. This is a weekly show where we hear from some of the industry's key figures who will advise on those key aspects of music marketing for music artists.

https://www.youtube.com/@AllAboutHelping/videos

Liberty Music PR

Find weekly tips and advice on what is hot in the music industry, and what is not. There is an emphasis on enabling independent artists to remain independent.

https://www.youtube.com/@libertymusicpr

Symphonic Distribution

Symphonic is probably one of the most securely backed music marketing channels as they are well-known for their distribution and video distribution service. Here, you will find help with distribution, royalty collection, marketing and much more.

https://www.youtube.com/@symphonicdistro

Music Money Makeover

Music Money Makeover has more of an emphasis on catering for record labels rather than artists, but this could be a good way to gain exposure for your own music too.

https://www.youtube.com/@MusicMoneyMakeover

Dark Music

Dark Music are a music distribution company who focus on supporting Indian music artists.

https://www.youtube.com/@darkmusicoriginal

HEATE

Heate is a big channel, but this is the first time it has come to our attention. They have taught well over 100,000 music producers to monetize their music and continue to publish great videos that enables you to achieve success in whatever way you define that in your music career.

https://www.youtube.com/@wegotthatHEATE

Musformation

Musformation is a channel run by Jesse Canon, a music nerd who helps you to promote your music with real-world advice and guidance from a true expert.

https://www.youtube.com/@Musformation

Music Gear Review Channels

MusicMarketingTV

Although the name would have you believe they operate a marketing channel, MusicMarketingTV is more of a gear review and gear tutorial channel. They will show you how to use various bits of kit like VST plugins, studio tools and much more.

https://www.youtube.com/@MusicMarketingTV

Chameleon Music Marketing Ltd

Chameleon Music Marketing focus on individual artists and bands. Again, they are more of an entertainment / review channel.

https://www.youtube.com/@ChameleonMusicMarketingLtd

MusicNGear

This channel has a particular focus on providing guitar reviews and unboxing videos.

https://www.youtube.com/@DominionFretWorks/

Boring Gear Reviews

I don't know how serious he was when he first named the channel, but this guy reviews guitars, as well as anything that has anything to do with guitars. If you love guitars, you'll feel right at home with this channel...

https://www.youtube.com/@boringgearreviews

Aaron Short Music

In his channel, Aaron promotes all things guitar. There are gear reviews, live performances and more. It also makes a refreshing change to hear an English accent. Check out Aaron Short Music...

https://www.youtube.com/@aaronshortmusic/

PAX Music

Find musical instrument reviews. PAX has reviewed a tonne of guitars, amps, ukelele as well as other videos on best Pinoy solos. PAX has a clear unique selling point in the fact that he does all of his videos in both Filipino and English.

https://www.youtube.com/@PAXmusicgearlifestyle

Music Magazine YouTube Channels

Bass Musician Magazine

Especially for bassists, as the name suggests, Bass Musician is a free online YouTube channel that helps bass players around the planet with on-the-go videos, gear reviews and Q&A sessions.

https://www.youtube.com/@BassMusicianMagazine

Talking Guitar: Jas Obrecht's Music Magazine

With a specific focus on blues guitar, Jas Obrecht focuses on American guitarists who have influenced the music scene throughout the twentieth century.

https://www.youtube.com/@TalkingGuitarJasObrecht/

HNM

Find mashups and remixes of many different artists.

https://www.youtube.com/@HNMMagazine

Sound on Sound

Sound on Sound is one of the oldest and most respected music magazines in the United Kingdom. It was established in 1985 so that fact in itself adds a good amount of authority to it. My own experience with Sound on Sound was particularly useful as I cited them in my University thesis.

https://www.youtube.com/@soundonsound

DIME Group

DIME Group is a music school, based in Detroit. However, they run courses across the USA and UK that are both campus-based and remote study. DIME offers University level courses in commercial music performance, commercial songwriting and music industry studies.

https://www.youtube.com/@dimedetroit

Computer Music Magazine

Learn everything you need to know about making music with your Mac and PC in this monthly magazine's YouTube channel. Some content that isn't available in the magazine is available on the YouTube channel. This includes tutorials, masterclasses by many accomplished musicians and gear reviews.

Music Radar

MusicRadar Tech provides a base for the video content to some of the top music magazines, Future Music and Computer Music, as well as those affiliated to MusicRadar. These include Electronic Musician, Keyboard Magazine, Guitarist, Guitar Techniques, Total Guitar and Bass Player.

https://www.youtube.com/@MusicRadarTech

Bedroom Producers Blog

In their own words, Bedroom Producers Blog is an online magazine about free free VST plugins, samples and loops.

https://www.youtube.com/@bpblog

Electronic Sound

Electronic Sound covers the lifespan of the synthesiser going back to the Kraftwerk years and before.

https://www.youtube.com/@ElectronicSound

Tutorial Services and Membership Sites

DK-MBA (Damian Keyes - Music Business Academy)

This is Damian's Music Business Academy. It is inexpensive, includes some great advice and it is obvious that Damian is a real expert in the business side of music.

On the negative side, Damian always assumes that we are singers. As I said above, we are not singers. We don't do that. However, it is interesting to have Damian's advice on DK0MBA.

https://www.dk-mba.com/

Sonic Academy

Sonic Academy as already mentioned in a previous chapter is an online learning resource for electronic music producers. They have new courses coming out on a weekly basis and plenty of great tutorials for you to watch on most DAWs.

The negative thing about Sonic Academy is that the vast majority of their courses are to do with Ableton. If you're not an Ableton user, you're already at a disadvantage. For me, I use FL Studio so I am not as well catered for.

Another great thing about Sonic Academy though, is they produce some fantastic products like Ana, Kick 2 and Node. I own all three of these synths.

https://www.sonicacademy.com/

Producertech

Producertech is an online resource that provides more in the way of hardware videos. If you own a Maschine as I do and you want to find some training so that you can get the best use of it, Producertech has the right courses.

New courses seem to be very sporadic on Producertech. If you are waiting for new courses to come in, you can be waiting a long time. Most DAW courses are concerned with Ableton too.

https://producertech.com/

Udemy

I probably have a record-breaking number of Udemy courses. This is mainly because I have used it as a currency to pay Alex for his mentoring. He used to ask me to buy a $10 course for 15 minutes of his time. I was happy to do this as Alex is a very experienced professional. I own around 200 Udemy courses.

I also own quite a few music courses on Udemy. Most of these concerns performance of one particular instrument or other. I have bought courses that include playing guitar, keyboards, bodhran and harmonica. I have also bought songwriting courses. If you are serious about a particular aspect of music, Udemy can be good.

If you pay for a course, you should see it through to the end. I haven't completed a lot of my courses. I have tended to get sidelined and not finished them. That, coupled with the fact that I paid for each course, is the negative point of buying Udemy courses. The vast majority of courses are never completed on Udemy by anyone who enrols.

https://www.udemy.com/

Point Blank Music School

Point Blank provide courses for students on a global scale. If you're in the UK or online, you will find degree courses. However, there are learning centres in Mumbai, China, Los Angles and Ibiza. You will find educational programmes that cover DJing, sound engineering, instrumentation and business subjects.

https://www.youtube.com/@PointBlankMusicSchool

ThinkSpace Education

ThinkSpace have a particular focus on writing music for the film, TV and games. They go up to Master's Degree level and courses are available for British students through Student Finance England.

https://youtube.com/@ThinkSpaceEducation

AMS Online

AMS Online was the company that I used to get my Master's Degree. The University of West London had the franchise for the Master's and I enjoyed my time with them.

https://www.youtube.com/@academyofmusicandsound3344

Stephen Ridley Academy

Although it is very expensive, the Ridley Academy has a terrific track record with teaching people from all walks of life to learn, play and perform piano with confidence.

https://www.youtube.com/@StephenRidleyTV

Music Blogs

WhatsOnRap.com

The following was sent over by WhatsOnRap.com

WhatsOnRap.com is a dedicated hip-hop blog that offers inspiration and support to emerging hip-hop and rap artists, especially those with limited budgets. Why should a rap or hip-hop newbie read my blog? My journey is proof that significant growth and impact can be achieved without a hefty budget. I've built this platform independently, relying solely on creativity, dedication, and a passion for the music industry.

As of Sunday, June 30, 2024, my blog has achieved remarkable milestones:
- Over 77k followers on Instagram
- More than 33k followers on Facebook
- 10k followers on Threads
- Over two million visits to the website since its inception

These achievements weren't made overnight. They are the result of consistent effort, strategic content creation, and genuine engagement with the hip-hop community. WhatsOnRap.com stands out because it offers authentic and relatable content that resonates with both newcomers and seasoned artists. The blog covers the latest trends and happenings in the rap game, ensuring that readers are both motivated and informed.

What's unique about WhatsOnRap.com is the hidden story behind its creation. While I may not explicitly share my personal journey on the blog, the story of how I built this platform with no financial investment is a testament to the power of perseverance and resourcefulness. By following my blog and social media channels, artists can see how one can creatively overcome obstacles and achieve significant milestones without a big budget.

While I am still working towards my ultimate goals and am not yet making significant money from this venture, my ongoing fight and progress are a testament to the power of perseverance. By following WhatsOnRap.com and my social media channels, artists can stay inspired and learn how to creatively overcome obstacles, just as I have.

In summary, WhatsOnRap.com is more than just a blog; it's a source of inspiration, a community, and a guide for hip-hop and rap artists who are striving to make their mark. I believe it will be a valuable addition to your book on music marketing, offering practical, real-world insights that resonate with artists from all genres.

Website: https://www.whatsonrap.com/

We Rave You

As you may gather from the name, WeRaveYou focuses on EDM and the continuation of the rave scene. There are several posts published each day.

Contact: general@weraveyou.com

Website: https://weraveyou.com

StereoFox

StereoFox puts the focus on the artist. I love this site after one visit. The love and respect that they show to the artist seems endless. They will cover different artists and review each of their songs. If I could give this top marks, I would

Contact: https://www.stereofox.com/contact//

Website: https://www.stereofox.com/

Louder Than War

Louder Than War has a focus on indie music that is up-to-date and interesting. There are often several posts per day and always at least one post per day. Louder Than War offers a great balance of interviews, features and reviews. If indie rock is your thing, you really need to investigate Louder Than War.

Contact:: davebeech@louderthanwar.com

Website: https://louderthanwar.com/

LouderThanWar also have a new artist section here - http://louderthanwar.com/contact/

This Song Is Sick

This Song is Sick covers single, EP and album reviews of electronic, indie rock and hip-hop. There are new posts every few days. However, there are a few publications on that day. For instance, there was three posts on the 13th July followed by three posts on the 16th. This is a terrific site, but if you wish to submit to it, you are going to have to contact them through X.com.

Contact: https://www.twitter.com/thissongissick_

Website: http://thissongissick.com/

Aquarium Drunkard

This is a site I visited recently. It is up-to-date and covers reviews on indie, contemporary and vintage music. There are typically two to three posts every day and they will post your music (no matter the genre) if it is good enough.

Contact: aquariumdrunkard@gmail.com

Website: http://www.aquariumdrunkard.com/

The Word is Bond

The Word is Bond delivers all things hip-hop with regular posts offering interest in the artists they support.

The Word is Bond will only publish your music if the cover art is good. They do have a submission guidelines page here - https://www.thewordisbond.com/wib-submission-guideline/

Contact: https://www.thewordisbond.com/wib-submissions-beta/

Website: https://www.thewordisbond.com/

Acid Stag

Acid Stag covers electronic music with several posts per day. Posts are delivered in a post feed format with all of the most recent posts being found after a pinned selection.

The submission guidelines for Acid Stage can be found at https://acidstag.com/about/

Contact: info@acidstag.com

Website: https://acidstag.com/

12XU

12XU covers punk rock and all posts are in German. If your fans understand German and you make punk rock music, you should give this one a shot.

Contact: http://onetwoxu.de/submissions/

Website: http://onetwoxu.de/

We All Want Someone to Shout For

Posts on We All Want Someone to Shout For look infrequent. However, there is a recent post which is why I included it. The site covers multiple different genres and are worth submitting your music to - even if it's only on the off chance.

We all want someone are very selective so your music must be good, but they are also open to any genre.

Contact: weallwantsomeone@gmail.com

Website: http://www.weallwantsomeone.org

Adobe and Teardrops

On first view, Adobe and Teardrops looks like posts are infrequent. There is a playlist from a couple of years ago that features quite prominently when you scroll down.

However, when you click on a post, you will find that the date is actually much more recent. The post I saw was from earlier this month. Therefore, it's worth trying to contact them if you make indie rock music.

Contact: ubia61@gmail.com

Website: http://www.adobeandteardrops.com

BuzzBands LA

BuzzBands LA covers the indie rock scene in Los Angeles, California. If this is something that your music can fit into, shoot them a submission and see if you can get some exposure from them.

Posts are infrequent - perhaps monthly. However, the most recent was earlier this month (July 2024).

Contact: kevin@buzzbands.la

Website: https://buzzbands.la/

A&R Factory

A&R Factory provides a focus on the development of new and aspiring artists. They cover reviews on alternative music and have a fresh and interesting appeal.

If you make alternative music, you are more than welcome to submit your music to them.

Contact: http://www.anrfactory.com/submit-demo/

Website: http://www.anrfactory.com/

High Clouds

High Clouds have a very impressive site with up-to-date posts. They are also very happy to consider music from a wide range of genres.

Submithub submissions are only accepted. They also have a focus on EP and album releases.

Contact:
https://www.submithub.com/blog/highclouds

Website: http://www.highclouds.org/

Kings of A&R

Kings of A&R has an appealing newspaper-style look with up-to-date posts. They consider music from multiple different genres so there is room for your music if you would like to contact them with a submission.

Contact: Dean@Kingsofar.com

Website: http://kingsofar.com/

The Music Ninja

The Music Ninja covers multiple genres and has new posts fairly frequently. From checking the website, it looks like new posts are delivered every couple of weeks. There also looks to be more of a focus on electronic music genres.

Contact: blas@themusicninja dot com

Website: http://www.themusicninja.com/

Pigeons & Planes

Pigeons & Planes is a well-known music blog that is all about hip-hop music. Posts are up-to-date with new content regularly.

Contact: submissions@pigeonsandplanes.com

Website: http://pigeonsandplanes.com/

Kane FM

Kane FM is a clear, flashy site with regular content updates. They will consider all genres of music so feel free to submit your music on the Contact page.

Contact: https://www.kanefm.com/contact/

Website: https://www.kanefm.com/

Surviving the Golden Age

Although the right toolbar would have you think that the site was well over 20 years old, there are some very recent posts so you should dig around before you leave the site.

Surviving the Golden Age supports artists from multiple different genres so there's your reason to submit your music.

Contact: https://survivingthegoldenage.com/about/submissions/

Website: http://survivingthegoldenage.com/

Wolf in a Suit

Wolf in a Suit is updated regularly and offers content on indie rock and indie pop.

The website is easy on the eyes and a pleasure to experience.

Contact: https://www.wolfinasuit.com/submit-music/ or email at thewolf@wolfinasuit.com

Website: http://www.wolfinasuit.com/

Channel Wavy

Channel Wavy covers reviews of multiple genres and updates daily. Posts could be a bit more spaced out with shorter paragraphs and larger font sizes, but it's well worth submitting your music to if you want to gain further exposure for your music.

Contact https://www.submithub.com/blog/channel-wavey

Website: http://channelwavy.com/

House Music With Love

With its interesting and fun design, House Music With Love was last updated recently. .

The site offers an enjoyable viewing experience and is worth submitting your music to if you make house music.
It should also be noted that House Music With Love operate a record label with a focus on deep house and techno.

Contact: demos@hmwl.org

Website: https://www.housemusicwithlove.com/

Asian Dan

Although it's not the most appealing site on the eye, the site has been updated a few times this month. Asian Dan posts reviews on experimental and electronic music.

Contact: asiandanblog@gmail.com

Website: https://asianmandan.com/

Pop Muzik

Pop Muzik a Swedish site with Swedish text. If that is ok for your music, why not shoot them a submission? As the name suggests, there is a focus on the pop music genres.

Popmuzik only accepts submissions through Submithub and all reviewed music is of songs that have been released less than one month ago.

Contact:
http://www.submithub.com/blog/popmuzik

Website: http://popmuzik.se/

For The Rabbits

For The Rabbits offers a grid wall of images with five things they have liked from the past week. Navigation is simple and all you need to do is hit the navigation bar in the top right corner. Why not shoot them a submission especially if you make indie music - whether that's independent music or indie rock is unclear. However, shoot them a submission and see if they like your music.

Contact: fortherabbitsmusic@gmail.com

Website: https://fortherabbits.net/

Tonspion.de

Tonspion is a German website and blog that covers all kinds of different music. Posts are up-to-date so if you have a following in Germany or if you're looking to increase your fanbase in Germany, Tonspion is an excellent opportunity for you to do so.

Contact:
https://www.submithub.com/blog/tonspion

Website: https://www.tonspion.de/

Purple Melon

Purple Melon has a similar layout to For the Rabbits which we covered a few moments ago. Posts are frequently updated and they will accept posts on popular music genres.

Contact: info@purplemelonmu.com

Website: https://purplemelonmu.com/

Indeflagration

Hope I just spelled that right. Indeflagration is a French site that offers reviews in French on multiple different genres of music. Music is posted sporadically with the last post being published this month at the time of writing. Even though they do post sporadically, it is well worth you sending them your submissions as you never know. They may feature your music.

Contact: contact@indeflagration.fr

Website: http://indeflagration.fr/

Planeta Pop

I believe Planeta Pop is probably Spanish. It covers all things pop music and is updated regularly. If you want to increase your Spanish fanbase, this is a fantastic opportunity for you to do just that.

Contact: planetapop@yahoo.com

Website: http://www.planetapop.com/

Under The Radar

Under The Radar are said to be supportive of multiple different genres. However, from the name and posts I have seen on the site, they look to be an underground music site so they will be promoting artists that many haven't heard of.

They are an up-to-date platform who post regularly and it is a joy to visit their well-designed website.

Contact: submissions@undertheradarmag.com

Website: https://www.undertheradarmag.com/

The Daily Listening

The Daily Listening have a specific focus on rock music. It should also be noted that The Daily Listening is a non-English language blog.

Contact: info@parapop.net

Website: https://www.thedailylistening.com/

BeatRoute Magazine

BeatRoute is a fun site with fun graphics and it delivers up-to-date industry news. They post at least once per week and sometimes twice. They are also happy to consider music of multiple different genres so shoot them your submission too.

There is more than one editor so when you submit your music, please make sure you contact the most appropriate one for your music.

Contact: http://beatroute.ca/contact-2/

Website: http://beatroute.ca/

Fingertips

First impressions of this site are that it is not very visually appealing. Paragraphs are long and don't really make you want to read them. It is also difficult to find new posts.

However, they do accept music from multiple different genres, but have more focus on rock and guitar-centric genres. If this is you, you should send them a submission.

Please note that Fingertips only shares free MP3s. You also need to follow the guidelines here: http://www.fingertipsmusic.com/?page_id=13

Contact: fingertipsmusic@gmail.com

Website: http://fingertipsmusic.com/

Umstrum

With regular posts reviewing music of multiple genres, Umstrum is another option that you should investigate.

The website is clearly set out and its bright and cheerful countenance bring a smile to your face.

Contact: http://umstrum.com/contact/

Website: http://umstrum.com/

Music Savage

Music Savage covers reviews on multiple different genres so shoot them your music and allow them a little time to consider it. They do update the blog regularly with fresh content. The website is also easy and clear to understand. BTW Music Savage would prefer you to contact them through Twitter.

Contact: http://www.twitter.com/musicsavage

Website: https://www.musicsavage.com

Earmilk

Earmilk is a blog that I have featured on Krannaken.com in the past in a blog roundup post. It's a great site and if you make music of any genre, you can send a submission to Earmilk for their consideration.

Contact: http://www.submithub.com/blog/earmilk

Website: https://earmilk.com/

Tuned Up

From visiting the website, I have an understanding that Tuned Up is more about guitar-centric music. However, I have heard that they are happy to review anything alternative so long as it sounds fantastic. Of course, they will only want the best music. Therefore, if you believe your tunes are good, send them.

Contact: http://iamtunedup.com/contact/

Website: http://iamtunedup.com/

Finest Ego

With Finest Ego, there is more of an emphasis on hip-hop, electronic and techno music genres. Therefore, if you make any of these genres, you can send them a submission for their consideration.

Contact: demos@finestego.com

Website: http://www.finestego.com/

Bolting Bits

Whatever genre your music is, you are welcome to forward it to Bolting Bits for their consideration. They post up-to-date reviews of multiple different genres and have a clear, easy-to-understand website that is very user-friendly.

Contact: contact@boltingbits.com

Website: http://boltingbits.com

The Ransom Note

The Ransom Note delivers music reviews covering multiple genres. They can also do interviews so if you want to gain more exposure, submit your music to them. The website is also quite flashy and feels easy and enjoyable to use.

Contact: info@theransomnote.co.uk

Website: http://www.theransomnote.com/

DJ Booth

Although the name might make you think more of electronic music genres, the mission of DJ Booth is actually to promote hip-hop. It has up-to-date posts and the site is well laid out. If you make hip-hop, you are welcome to submit it.

Contact: http://www.submithub.com/blog/djbooth

Website: http://djbooth.net/

Conclusion

All the strategies in this book will enable you to market your music more successfully. However, I recommend that you only use the strategies and ideas that lead to your goal. For instance, some of you will not want fame. Furthermore, some of you will not want to travel and have your name and life story shared with the media.

My advice is to have your end goal in mind throughout your career. Therefore, your end goal should be included in your business plan at the very beginning.

The reason I included the chapter on preparing your business plan at the very start, is because it is the most important document you are going to have to write. However, you can and should change your business plan as you proceed through your career.

These days, it is not good enough to just say, "I want to make money in music". There is so much to do in this industry. You may find yourself helping other artists (as is the aim of this book).

I hope you have enjoyed reading this book and that you can take these strategies and make your music a success.

Go through the book chapter by chapter along with me, the author, in a weekly course where you can ask me all of your burning questions about music marketing. Learn more at...

https://www.patreon.com/KrannakenMusicBlog

Printed in Great Britain
by Amazon